MW01145296

ARIZONA SUMMITS

SOUTH

A Guide to Mountains, Peaks, and High Points

by Tyler Williams

Funhog Press
Flagstaff, Arizona

Overview map

Northern Arizona

Mogollon Rim

Harquahala Mtn.

Mazatzal Pk.

Big Horn Pk.

Piestewa Pk.

Mt. Ord

Aztec Pk.

Eagle Tail Pk.

Camelback Mtn.

Browns Pk.

Signal Pk.

Weavers Needle

Woolsey Pk.

South Mtn.

Pinals

Castle Dome Pk.

Montezuma Pk.

Phoenix

Pinalenos

Window Pk.

Picacho Pk.

Mt. Lemmon

Bassett Pk.

Cathedral Rk.

Dos Cabezas

Mt. Ajo

Wasson Pk.

Tucson

Kitt Pk.

Rincon Pk.

Cochise Head

Baboquivari

Mt. Wrightson

Chiricahua Crest

Miller Pk.

Alphabetical List of Routes

ARIZONA SUMMITS

SOUTH

Tyler Williams

Funhog Press

Disclaimer

Hiking, mountain climbing, and peak bagging are dangerous activities. Other dangerous actions associated with exploring mountains include, but are not limited to: driving to trailheads, camping far from well-lit streets, walking over uneven terrain, scrambling, and climbing. If you don't want to endanger your life, please do not use this book.

Nature is constantly changing. Landslides obliterate trails, rockfalls destroy routes, vegetation covers paths. Additionally, legal jurisdictions and human attitudes change, resulting in closed trailheads and blocked access roads. Therefore, any information contained herein should be considered out of date, and quite possibly incorrect.

The author and publisher of *Arizona Mountains—South* claims no responsibility for any actions taken through the use of this book. As a living being on this planet, you are burdened with the responsibility to take care of yourself regardless of any circumstances that might occur beyond your control. No amount of guidance, either from a guidebook or otherwise, can replace personal judgement.

PRINTED IN USA

Published by Funhog Press
www.funhogpress.com

ISBN 0-9664919-5-5

Edited by Lisa Gelczis, Alison Govi
Designed by Mary Williams www.marywilliamsdesign.com
Cover photos by Tyler Williams
Photos by Tyler Williams, Lisa Gelczis

Table of Contents

Book Origins

I've spent much of my life exploring the bottoms of the earth—rappelling down narrow gorges, and paddling deep river canyons. The clandestine feel of chasms has always been an attraction, but equally appealing is the way drainages connect the landscape. By traveling from the head of a river system, through its life stages and past its various tributaries to join a central artery of the whole, I am able to link the geography of a region. This game of "connecting the dots" is one of my primary motivations for exploring wild places.

Thus, it isn't much of a leap for me to go from the depths to the summits. How better to piece together the puzzle of geography than by standing atop a lofty viewpoint and surveying a great swath of landscape? Besides, few things are as satisfying as looking at an eminent peak, and then finding a way to its top. Surely a committed funhog such as myself would find his way, eventually, to the rocky heights.

So, when I discovered that no current guidebook existed exclusively for the mountain peaks of Arizona, it wasn't long before the idea made the top of my project list. But this book is hardly the first of its kind. That honor goes to Bob and Dotty Martin, who published *Arizona's Mountains* in 1991.

The Martins retired in Tucson, and proceeded to exhaustively explore Arizona's high points. The couple described 175 different mountain routes in their book, and made it to the top of many more. Their tome is a great resource for Arizona exploration, and this book is based in large part on that thorough guide. I used Bob and Dotty's descriptions to seek most of the routes you'll find in this book. I owe them a great deal.

This book is slightly different in scope than that one, however. While the Martins concentrated on high elevation points within the state, the focus of *Arizona Summits* was to chronicle the most striking, prominent, important, outrageous, and enjoyable summit routes I could find. My loose criteria for choosing routes often unwittingly led to county high points and several top-listed peaks, but as you'll discover, the selection process clearly favored beautiful lines, easy access, and overall impressiveness. Elevation was less important than inspiration.

Elevation also played a role in limiting the book to the southern half of the state. If a book were based on simply the highest mountains, Northern Arizona and the White Mountains would dominate the text, neglecting the striking ranges of southern Arizona. This brought the realization that there were more outstanding summits out there than would fit practically into one book. The Arizona Summits concept broke into smaller pieces. *Arizona Summits—South* is the product. A version for the north half of the state is forthcoming, assuming of course, that y'all buy enough copies of this book to keep the Funhog life raft afloat.

R-E-S-P-E-C-T

Many of our natural areas are negatively impacted from human visitation. Low impact camping, hiking, climbing, or just plain living can generally be summed up by one simple word: RESPECT. If we pay attention and respect the world around us, our presence as backcountry travelers is less impactful, regulations are less necessary, and our experiences are more pleasant. Below are a few tips that might help us treat the environment with proper, logical respect.

1) Observe wildlife quietly and from a distance. The most rewarding wildlife watching occurs when animals are acting naturally.

2) Be careful with micro-trash. Although most peak baggers aren't stupid enough to leave their discarded case of beer smoldering in the fire ring, we do sometimes lose track of the small stuff. Make a camp sweep whenever you leave an area to check for anything left behind.

3) Be careful to not roll rocks. Rockfall is not only dangerous, it causes excessive erosion. Do your best to travel lightly across the land.

4) Crap carefully. Go at least a couple hundred feet from water, and get well off any trails before taking a dump. Bury your feces. If the substrate is too hard to dig a hole, find a rock that you can lift, poop under it, and place it back as it was. Pack out your toilet paper. A ziploc bag works fine for this purpose. If you can't pack it out, burn it—without starting a forest fire! Or better yet, don't use any toilet paper in the first place. A smooth rock, stick, or leaf (not poison ivy!) works nearly as well as TP. Lighten up and get back to basics.

Acknowledgements

Many have contributed invaluably to this book. My mother's indomitably positive spirit has helped me initiate every book project I've undertaken, including this one. My father's competitiveness and pride are constant reminders to keep going when I don't want to. My wife, Lisa, is a stalwart summit hiking partner, photographer, model, editor, consultant, business manager, friend, and much much more. Funhog Press would not exist without her. I owe my friend Orea Roussis credit for suggesting that I narrow the scope of my Arizona Summits project into two halfs, at least. This book would not have come to fruition without her advice. As always, Donita Polly at USGS was a friendly face and an accommodating assistant with my map research. Rob and Marguerite at Pinnacle Mapping Services came through huge in my quest for digital topos. Andy Martin helped by answering prominence questions and providing his County High Points book. Thank you sponsors: Gareth at Osprey Packs, Jason at Asolo, and Stephen and Peter at Teva. Mary Williams was again a star at cover design and book layout, besides tutoring her technologically challenged cousin in the latest computer tricks. Finally, thanks to my buds who accompanied me on my summit quests; Govi, Phillips, Gelczis, and Ruth Grande.

An explanation of the header catagories

General Description
This is a brief overview of the route.

Summit Elevation
The elevation of the featured mountain or high point. In most cases, this figure is taken from United States Geological Survey topographic maps. In some cases, the figure is taken from USGS summit benchmarks, if they differ from the map.

Vertical Gain
The total vertical between the route's start and the summit. In cases where significant vertical loss is encountered along the route, all vertical gains are totaled.

Round-Trip Distance
This is the total round-trip distance of the route described.

Optimal Season
This is generally the best season for the route described. This is not to say it is the only season for a particular route. A winter traverse of the Chiricahua Crest, for example, could be a great adventure for someone with the necessary skills, but it is not what most of us would consider optimal. Likewise, a summertime outing to a low elevation peak like Camelback Mountain is possible, even commonplace, but hardly ideal.

Route Surface and Difficulty
This category evolved during the research phase of the book as I explored Arizona's mountains with different hiking partners. It became apparent that the specific surface underfoot (or under wheel) made a vast difference to each individual's hiking style and ability. The category is intended to describe the ground surface along a given route. When several route surfaces occur, each is listed in order of appearance en route to the summit.

Summit Seasons

Summiting in southern Arizona spans the seasons. Late autumn through winter is an ideal time to explore the low desert ranges in the state's southwestern quadrant. Although occasional patches of snow might occupy shady nooks on the highest peaks, rarely does it accumulate enough to present a hazard. By March the sun is already burning high overhead, creating uncomfortably warm hiking conditions at elevations below 4,000 feet. As spring progresses through April, mountains between 5,000' and 7,000' gradually clear of snow. Roads open, trails dry, and routes to the peaks become less slick. June is an excellent time to visit the highest summits, as elevations over 8,000 feet provide a welcome respite from the stifling heat of the Sonoran Desert. Arizona's sky islands can occasionally be idyllic during summer, but the monsoon season of July through mid-September often brings cold rain and dangerous lightning to the mountain tops. Start early and be ready to bail in an instant if you venture to the high peaks during this season. On the whole, October is the most accommodating time in southern Arizona's mountains. November is often an excellent month for peak bagging before December's cold and snow shuts down the high peaks, and the summit season for the low desert ranges begins anew.

Arizona—all seasons all the time

Climbing Rating Systems

In this book, some routes are simple hiking, a few are technical rock climbs, and many fall somewhere in between. Based on a European mountaineers' system developed in the 1920s, a class 1 to 5 rating system exists encompassing everything from trail hiking to overhanging rock climbs. Below is an explanation of the five classes as they are used in this book.

Class 1: Trail hiking. No hands are needed to proceed. A fall will not generate any downhill movement.

Class 2: Rough trail or off-trail hiking. Hands might be used for balance. A fall will produce a slight downhill slide.

Class 3: Scrambling. Hands are often needed for balance and propulsion. A fall will be exasperated by the steepness of the slope.

Class 4: Scrambling and easy climbing. Hands are definitely needed. A fall will usually cause injury. Ropes are useful.

Class 5: Climbing. Hands and fingers are needed to proceed. A fall will almost always cause injury, or death. Ropes are always used, except for the most skillful and daring climbers.

Class 5 is further divided by decimal points from 5.0 to (presently) 5.15. A 5.0 climb is equivalent to a vertical ladder. A 5.1 climb has half the rungs missing. A 5.2 climb has the remaining rungs sawed in half. A 5.3 climb has half the remaining rungs sawed in half again, and so on. A 5.15 climb includes only the vague memory of a ladder, and even Spiderman would pause.

Class 1

Some need to pray to the sun at high noon, need to howl at the midwinter moon.
Reborn and baptized in a moment of grace.
Just need a break from the headlong race...

NP

Class 2

Class 3

Class 4

Class 5

Navigation and GPS

Navigating through mountainous terrain can be difficult. I have done my best to explain the routes in this book accurately, but there will no doubt be cases in which potential summiters stand lost amid a cactus sea, book in hand, cursing my name. Suffering the wrath of this scorn is an inevitable (and inenviable) part of writing guidebooks. Nonetheless, for this book I have tried to mitigate the confusion through the use of technology, sort of.

GPS (Global Positioning System) units are now as common on backcountry trails as maps used to be. Whether hikers are more or less often lost remains a mystery. GPS units can provide a false sense of security for those unfamiliar with backcountry travel. Like any technology, GPS units are only as good as the person using them. In featureless environments like the ocean, open plains, or flat dense forests, GPS units are invaluable. In mountainous environments where topography is paramount, however, GPS units are often little more than unecessary extra weight. Better to rely on map reading skills and your own backcountry senses in most of Arizona's mountain country. Of course the best scenario for staying found includes a good map, a sense of the terrain, a GPS, *and* a good guidebook.

GPS coordinates are listed in this book by latitude and longitude. **Datum used is NAD 83**. Coordinates are used mostly for trailhead locations so that those who have left work on a Friday afternoon are able to find the parking spot in the dark. In some cases, I have indicated GPS coordinates for essential junctions along nebulous summit routes, but I have kept this practice to a minimum. The more technology we bring into the wilderness, the more we tarnish the experience we are there to seek. I leave my GPS home on most outings. You shouldn't need one to explore the routes in this book. But it might help.

A Word About Maps

Before attempting any summit beyond a beaten trail, one should know a little something about map reading. The descriptions within this book sometimes reference printed elevations found on topographic maps. Without a good map, staying found can be a dubious proposition.

The maps in *Arizona Summits* are intended to be used wtih detailed topographic maps of an area. Although routes have been drawn meticulously on the maps within this book, the scale constraints of a guidebook make them inadequate for sole use in the field. To locate the routes and reach the summits listed in this book, one should read the descriptions, reference the guidebook maps, and bring a full size topographic map into the field with them.

What the Hell is Prominence?

Prominence describes the relative elevation of a mountain summit. Mountains have long been recognized for their elevations above sea level. This single calculation, however, doesn't reflect a peak's height over the surrounding terrain, and is therefore not a true conveyance of a particular landform's importance. A true measure of a mountain's size is better represented by a calculation called prominence.

If a mountain is 15,000 feet above sea level, but it sits on a 14,000' foot-high plateau, it's rise isn't very impressive—only 1,000 feet of prominence. If that same 15,000' high mountain rises from a plain only 5,000 feet-high, it will be a seriously tall mountain—one with 10,000 feet of prominence.

Seattle mountaineer Steve Fry coined the term "prominence" in the early 1980s, and sub-cultures of mountain enthusiasts have since developed innumerable lists and theories surrounding the concept. In Great Britan, summiters have assigned a prominence rating to nearly every hill in the country. Here in the American Southwest, documentation is less thorough, but many lists still exist. Check the back of this book for a few of them.

Basically, prominence measures how eminent, or prominent, a mountain is. Specifically, prominence has been defined as: The elevation of a summit relative to the highest point to which one must descend before reascending to a higher summit. In other words, a mountain's prominence is measured to the highest saddle below the summit before the terrain rises to a higher summit.

Southern Arizona has no peaks over 12,000' in elevation, but it contains four landforms that break the 5,000' prominence mark—a benchmark figure in mountain measurement. Five additional summits in Southern Arizona penetrate the 4,000' prominence level, and many others boast impressive verticals in the 3,000' range. Mt. Graham, the high point of the Pinaleno Mountains, has 6,340' of prominence, ranking it as the most prominent mountain in Arizona, and the twentieth most prominent mountain in the United States.

DRIVES

South Mountain

DRIVE

General Description: A paved road through a desert preserve
Summit Elevation: 2,630'
Vertical Gain: 1,360'
Round-Trip Distance: 15 miles from the park entrance to Gila Vista
Optimal Season: Anytime
Route Surface and Difficulty: Paved road

The escarpment of South Mountain is perhaps the Valley's most recognizable landmark. For decades, the winding road that leads up the mountain has exposed the wonders of mountaintops to a variety of Arizonans. Officially titled the Guadalupe Mountains, the range is nonetheless known by most as South Mountain, because it lies to the south of downtown Phoenix.

There are a couple of places on the way up the mountain that allow parking, but spaces are limited, so driving up the mountain is generally a nonstop curving ascent through a Sonoran desertscape. About 2 miles from the entrance station, the road forks. If you are summit-bound, bear left here on San Juan Road.

The San Juan Road makes a gradual climb up the north slopes of the mountain before reaching a saddle at mile 3.6, where there is some parking available to access hiking trails. About 2 miles farther on, there is a T intersection. Turning left here will take you to the Dobbins Lookout.

Looking directly down on central Phoenix, this is the most popular vista on the mountain. There are picnic tables, a stone ramada, and a small kiosk with arrows pointing out various geographical features of the Valley. Views to the north include the Mazatzal and Bradshaw Mountains.

To gain even broader views from the top of the mountain, return past the T intersection and continue beyond the Buena Vista spur road at mile 6.1, veering right toward the Gila Valley Vista. The road winds another 1.4 miles through a garden-like desert basin before reaching the top.

The actual summit of South Mountain is closed to the public due to the presence of radio and television towers, but the parking area at the Gila Vista offers a better view to the south anyway. The Sierra Estrellas dramatically rise just a few miles away across the pancake-flat Gila Valley. Table Top Mountain is the highest peak in the middle distance to the south. You might recognize it. It looks like a table top. Farther east is the distinctive dome of the Santa Catalina Mountains near Tucson. On a good day, the profile of Picacho Peak can be seen through the low desert haze. The Superstition Mountains are not far to the east, just beyond the development of southern Mesa, Arizona.

Sonoran Desert cruisin'

Access: Exit Interstate 10 at Baseline Road. Head west about 6 miles to Central Avenue and turn south. In a little over a mile, the road enters the foothills of South Mountain. About 2 miles from Baseline Road, you will enter South Mountain Regional Park.

South Mountain's Dobbins Lookout and downtown Phoenix, AZ

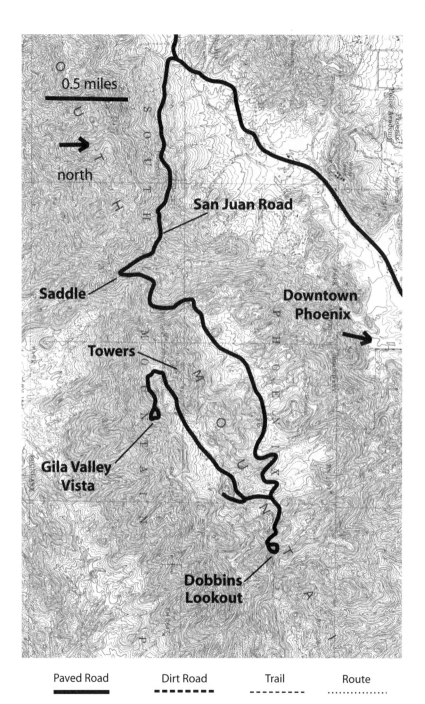

0.5 miles

north

San Juan Road

Saddle

Towers

Downtown
Phoenix

Gila Valley
Vista

Dobbins
Lookout

| Paved Road | Dirt Road | Trail | Route |

Pinal Mountain

DRIVE

General Description: A dirt road drive to the top of a central Arizona high point
Summit Elevation: 7,848'
Vertical Gain: 4,200' from Globe
Round-Trip Distance: 23 miles on dirt / 28 miles round-trip from Globe
Optimal Season: April — November / Snow necessitates a road closure in winter.
Route Surface and Difficulty: Good dirt road with some narrow spots

The Pinal Mountains perch on the edge of the Sonoran Desert near the town of Globe, Arizona. Viewed from afar, the range is more of a single mountain than an entire range, hence the common name of Pinal Mountain. When one travels up the mountain, however, he will see that there are a collection of ridges and canyons here, along with two distinct summits, Signal Peak and Pinal Peak. Given this closer perspective, Pinal "Mountain" is evident as the diverse mountain range that it truly is.

To ascend the slopes of this range, find your way to forest road #55 (see logistics) where the surface turns to dirt, and national forest lands begin. The road climbs slopes above an ephemeral creek, leaving the homes of Globe behind. About a mile past the end of the pavement, road #651 branches left at the top of a hill. This is the fork leading to the summit, cutting across slopes of thick central Arizona chaparral.

The chaparral gives way to forest rather abruptly as ponderosa pine and Emory oak envelops the road shortly after the fork. The road winds up one of the mountain's many canyons, with a few small turnouts that allow access to an idyllic creek setting complete with ancient arching sycamore trees.

A little over 6 miles from the pavement, road #651 breaks out of the canyon and bears left at a pass. There is a pull-out just beyond this fork at the pass, offering open views as forest is again exchanged for chaparral on the southwest facing slopes of the mountain.

The next couple miles require the most focused driving of the route, because road #651 twists along steep exposed slopes where there is often no room for two vehicles to pass. Things improve when the road breaks over a ridge back to north facing terrain, and the forests return. At this elevation, there is not only ponderosa pine, but also Southwestern white pine, Douglas fir, and Gambel oak.

When the road splits at a junction of #651 and #651 N, stay left for Signal and Pinal Peaks. Almost 11 miles after leaving pavement, there is a

Stairway to Heaven?

gated road leading to Signal Peak on the right. This gated road can make a nice 1 mile round-trip hike to an old summit lookout tower.

Continuing on #651, you'll enter the Pinal Mountain Recreation Area in less than a quarter-mile. Within the recreation area, the road runs through a quaint mountaintop forest, home to a campground and a number of summer cabins. Once beyond the roadside cabins, #651 finally reaches the high point of the Pinal Mountains at Pinal Peak.

The summit is somewhat anticlimactic, with no single 360° view and a crowd of communication towers. For the true high point, seek out a granite boulder at the north end of the summit area. For the best views, walk or drive out to two other promontories nearby.

By exploring different vantage points, you will be able to spot many Arizona landmarks including the low notched bulge of the White Mountains to the northeast, the Santa Teresa mountains nearby to the east, and the Pinalenos beyond. The Galiuro Mountains are the next low range spanning southwestward before the double hump of the Rincons and Santa Catalinas rise prominently above the low desert. On most days, a discerning eye will be able to pick out Picacho Peak in the lowlands to the southwest. Views of the Superstitions, Mazatzals, and Mogollon Rim can be had from the summit of nearby Signal Peak.

Access: From downtown Globe, take Broad Street south to a stop sign at the railroad tracks. Turn right onto Jesse Hayes Road past Connie's Market, and continue 0.8 miles to Ice House Canyon Road. Go right on Ice House Canyon Road, then right again at a stop in about 1.5 miles onto road #55 toward Pinal Peak. In 2 miles, this paved road turns to graded dirt and enters the Tonto National Forest.

You can also reach Jesse Hayes Road by turning directly off Highway 60 on the east side of the Pinal Creek railroad overpass in Globe. There is a sign here for Pinal Mountain Recreation Area and Besh Ba Gowah Archaeological Park. About 100 yards from Highway 60, turn right on Broad Street, then make a quick left onto Jesse Hayes Road.

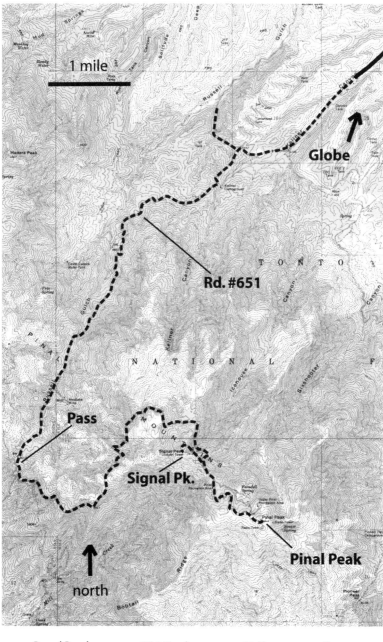

1 mile

Rd. #651

Globe

Pass

Signal Pk.

Pinal Peak

north

Paved Road   Dirt Road   Trail   Route

Aztec Peak

DRIVE

General Description: A drive to the high point of the Sierra Anchas
Summit Elevation: 7,748'
Vertical Gain: 2,345' from Young Highway to summit
Round-Trip Distance: 14 miles from Young Highway
Optimal Season: April — November
Route Surface and Difficulty: One-lane rocky road, exposed in one location, suitable for high clearance two-wheel-drives

The Sierra Anchas are the quintessential central Arizona mountain range. Rising from saguaro cactus to ponderosa pines, the mountains encompass cliff-bound gorges, clear perennial streams, chaparral rangeland, and clandestine ancient ruins. The high point of the range, Aztec Peak, has had a lookout tower on top since the 1950s. The tower is one of several fire lookouts that once provided summer employment and back-of-beyond inspiration for Western luminary Edward Abbey.

To reach the summit of Aztec Peak, and perhaps gain your own bit of Abbey-esque inspiration, leave the Young Highway (route 288) at Workman Creek, turning onto road #487 near milepost 284. Initially, road #487 runs through a lush forest that thrives along the canyon bottom of Workman Creek. About 2.5 miles from Young Highway, the road steepens and narrows before traversing crumbling cliffs adjacent to Workman Creek Falls—a dramatic cascade during times of high water.

The road improves above the falls, but it continues to climb. Curving through a dense post-burn forest of locust, maple, and oak, the route is more reminiscent of an Appalachian country road than an Arizona byway. When road #487 flattens onto the range highlands, deciduous thickets give way to park lands of bracken fern, oak, and scattered pine. Just over 6 miles from the Young Highway, stay left at a fork for the final climb to the summit.

Less than fifty steps up the lookout tower will reveal a sweeping view of central Arizona. To the south, the Four Peaks cut a sawtoothed horizon above the waters of Theodore Roosevelt Reservoir. The crest of the Four Peaks, and the Mazatzal Range to which they belong, can be traced northwesterly, disappearing briefly behind nearby Carr Peak before reemerging at tower-adorned Mt. Ord. A gap in the range just north of Mt. Ord allows a view to the distant Bradshaw Mountains. The Mazatzals continue to stairstep northward, terminating at rounded North Peak where the range plunges to the depths near the confluence of the Verde and East Verde Rivers. In the

En route to the Sierra Ancha's high point via Young Highway

foreground, the forested basin of Workman Creek feeds the gorges of upper Salome Creek.

To the northwest, the flattened nipple of Baker Butte signals a high point along the Mogollon Rim, which runs in a long continuous swath across the northern horizon. In the northeast, the Rim becomes a many-knolled landscape. These rounded bumps are cinder cones of the northern White Mountains volcanic field. The horizon gently rises eastward to a vague double hump at the Rim's high point—the aptly named White Mountains. Between your vantage point on Aztec Peak and the Whites, the upper Salt River hides beneath buttressed terrain, most of which lies within the Apache Indian Reservation.

The usually hazy Gila River Valley occupies a low spot in the viewscape southeastward, with the rim of Mt. Graham and the Pinalenos perching above the Gila valley to the south. The mines at Globe appear as a light splotch, with the Pinal Mountains looming behind. On clear days, the Santa Catalina Mountains can be glimpsed through a saddle in the Pinals.

More mining activity near Miami, Arizona, is blatantly obvious in the south, where a uniform slope of bright slag scourges a panoply of dark blue hills. The jagged Superstition Mountains cut the horizon to the southwest, leading the eye back to the Four Peaks.

Access: Take Highway 88 / 188 north from Globe, AZ for about 15 miles to the junction of Highway 288—Young Highway. Take the Young Highway (288) north for 26 miles, climbing from the Salt River, past dramatic Parker Creek Canyon, and into the pine forests of the Sierra Anchas. At milepost 284.1, turn onto forest road #487 and follow it for 7 miles to the summit of Aztec Peak.

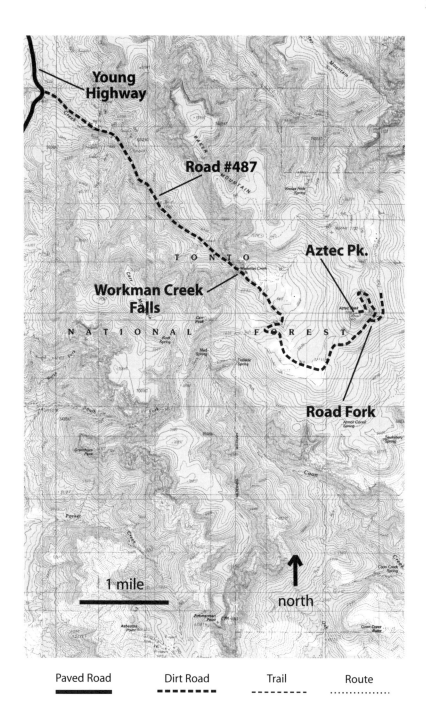

Young Highway

Road #487

Aztec Pk.

Workman Creek Falls

Road Fork

1 mile

north

Paved Road   Dirt Road   Trail   Route

Mount Ord

DRIVE / HIKE

General Description: A dirt road drive to an overlook, with an optional short hike to the summit of Mt. Ord
Summit Elevation: 7,128'
Vertical Gain: 2,250' from Highway 87 to overlook / 378' from overlook to summit
Round-Trip Distance: 12 miles driving / 1.5 miles hiking to summit
Optimal Season: April — October
Route Surface and Difficulty: One-and-a-half-lane dirt road with some rocky sections

Mt. Ord is a beautifully shaped conical peak located smack in the middle of the Mazatzal Mountains, a range composed of Precambrian metamorphic and igneous rocks. In other words, Mazatzal rocks are hard, and the mountains are old. They were once quite high too. Gravel deposits of Mazatzal origin have been found north of the Mogollon Rim, indicating to geologists that Mazatzal streams once drained from the high Mazatzals onto the lower Rim country. This all occurred about 50 million years ago, before drainages like Tonto Creek cut valleys that now separate the Rim from the central ranges.

The ancient Mazatzals have since eroded, leaving the precipitous range we know today. The only place one can drive to a summit within the range is here at Mt. Ord, where a collection of communication towers necessitates a maintained road leading to the top. The last 0.7 miles of road is closed to vehicles, but the summit can be reached on foot. If you are not able to make the walk to the towers, several viewpoint picnic spots near the end of the public road still serve as worthy destinations.

From the highway, the Mt. Ord road is paved for the first half-mile, then it turns into a rocky dirt track a lane-and-a-half wide. About 2 miles from the highway, the route narrows to a single lane as it unnervingly traverses a steep hillside where a slip off the side would send you tumbling to the depths. Fortunately, the exposed section only lasts for a half-mile. Higher up the mountain, occasional eroded gullies require a slow steady foot on the accelerator, but the road is certainly passable to two-wheel-drive vehicles during dry conditions.

About 5 miles from the highway, there is a wide pull-out offering a rest stop as the road winds around the north side of the mountain. At 5.5 miles from the highway, the road enters a basin of pines and stout sweeping oaks. Once gaining the ridgetop at 6,730' at mile 6, the road is blocked by a

Walkin' down a country road on Mt. Ord

gate. Parking areas exist nearby.

Excellent views are available adjacent to the road gate. Below to the south, Highway 87—The Beeline Highway (so named because it makes a beeline to the high country) crosses Sycamore Creek via a divided bridge. Adjacent to the bridge is the tiny community of Sunflower. Maverick and Granite Mountains rise behind Sunflower to the north and south respectively, with the valley of the lower Verde River behind. The McDowell Mountains rise on the far side of the Verde. Beyond the McDowells, greater Phoenix hides in the haze, with the Sierra Estrella Mountains cutting the skyline on the far side of the city.

Blue waters of Bartlett Lake are visible along the lower Verde River. White towers atop Humboldt Mountain can be spotted northwest of the lake. Farther west and north, the high blue Bradshaw Mountains rise above the lower ranges. The view to the north is dominated by the northern Mazatzals, with stair-stepped Mazatzal Peak reigning as the highest point in the range.

If you care to reach the summit of Mt. Ord, it is a 0.75 mile walk and 380' vertical feet up the road. At the top, there is a closed lookout tower and an array of highly charged communication equipment, not exactly a great place for a picnic. More landmarks can be seen than from the gate below, however. The Tonto Basin and Roosevelt Lake lie to the east, and a keen eye will spot the very tip of Weavers Needle in the Superstition Mountains.

Access: Take Highway 87 north from Mesa about 30 miles to the Mazatzal Range divide. At milepost 222.7, turn east onto paved Mt. Ord Road #626.

#626 traverses slopes below the peak

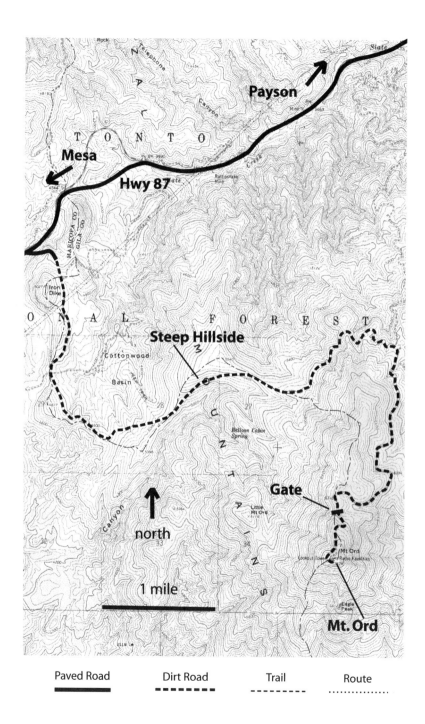

Paved Road   Dirt Road   Trail   Route

Pinaleno Mountains

DRIVE / HIKE

General Description: A drive up Arizona's top-ranked mountain in prominence, with hiking options to a lookout
Summit Elevation: Mt. Graham—10,720' / Heliograph Pk.—10,028'
Vertical Gain: 6,972' from Safford to the Heliograph Pk. summit
Round-Trip Distance: 44 miles (22 miles one-way) on road to Heliograph Peak fire road / 4 miles to hike up the dirt road to the Heliograph summit
Optimal Season: mid-April — mid-November / In heavy snow years the road can be closed through April.
Route Surface and Difficulty: Curvy paved road / gravel road for hiking

The Swift Trail leading into the Pinaleno Mountains is a classic Arizona road. Winding uphill, first across old lake sediments (the Safford Valley was once under a big lake), and then up slopes of the mountain via steep switchbacks, the road traverses an array of life zones.

First there are the desert grasslands of the valley, then oak woodlands of the lower slopes, and finally conifer forests on the upper mountain. Of course this is a gross generalization of the many biotic communities encountered by ascending over a vertical mile, but suffice to say, even an ecotone neophyte will notice big changes in their surroundings on a drive up the Swift Trail.

About 6 miles from Highway 191, there is a road on the right that leads 1 mile to a great overlook of the Gila River Valley. At 7.2 miles, the road reaches the Noon Creek Picnic Area, so named because prior to the automobile, travelers generally arrived here for a midday break in their horse drawn ride up the mountain. Turkey Flat, at mile 14, is a forested benchland with a cluster of summer cabins. The elevation here is 7,500'.

The road continues through a series of sharp turns and long ascents as it approaches Ladybug Saddle at mile 17. This makes a good rest stop before the road breaks over to the south side of the range, and into a more open landscape of stolid windblown pines. The first good overlook along the main road doesn't come until mile 21.8. It is on the left, across from Shannon Campground.

This is the summit ridge of the Pinaleno Mountains, where the waters of east-flowing Marijilda Wash meet those of west-draining Big Creek. The view from the overlook frames the Sulphur Springs Valley with its sweeping grasslands and center-pivot irrigation. The Winchester Mountains sit on the far side of the valley. In the distance, the distinctive nipple of Mt. Wrightson rises above a mountain saddle. The Rincons and Santa Catalinas appear as

Scanning 7,000 vertical from Heliograph Peak

a single mountain with two summits from this angle. Farther north are the gently rising Galiuro Mountains.

Shortly beyond this overlook, the road is closed to motorized vehicles from November 15 to April 15, or longer during big snow winters. In summer, you can drive another 13 miles on dirt to the end of the road, with a few nice overlooks along the way. The high point of the Pinaleno Mountains, known as Mt. Graham or High Peak, is permanently closed. A massive telescope now occupies that part of the mountain, while Mt. Graham red squirrels run unmolested in the dying forest below.

Across from the Shannon overlook back at mile 21.8, the gated Heliograph Peak Road can provide a nice walk. Hiking the closed road takes one through a forest of Southwestern white pine, white fir, and some of Arizona's largest Douglas firs.

At the summit there is an historic lookout cabin, and the lookout itself. Heliograph Peak was named for heliographs (mirrors for communicating with Morse code) that the United States cavalry used here during the subjugation of the Apache people in the late 1800s.

Today, an expansive view of the Apache's homeland remains. The broad low hump of the White Mountains (and Mt. Baldy) is visible to the north / northeast. Blue Peak is identifiable as a small knob atop the Mogollon Rim farther to the southeast. The Phelps Dodge mines are obvious in the middle distance, with the Mogollon Mountains of New Mexico rising behind and to the right. The nearby Chiricahua Mountains are in the southeast, with the similar shapes of Cochise Head and Dos Cabezas sitting between the Chiricahuas and Heliograph Peak.

Access: From Safford, head south on Highway 191 toward Willcox. About 6 miles out of town, turn west on Highway 366—the Swift Trail. This junction is at mile 113.7 on Highway 191.

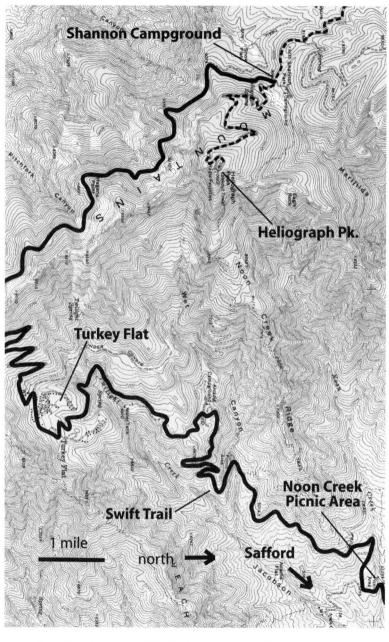

Shannon Campground

Heliograph Pk.

Turkey Flat

Noon Creek Picnic Area

Swift Trail

Safford

1 mile

north ➤

| Paved Road | Dirt Road | Trail | Route |

Mount Lemmon

DRIVE

General Description: A drive up a scenic paved road, with an optional short hike to an overlook
Summit Elevation: 9,157'
Vertical Gain: 6,300' from the valley floor
Round-Trip Distance: 55 miles from the valley to the summit and back
Optimal Season: April — November
Route Surface and Difficulty: Paved road / secondary paved road with potholes / optional trail with loose cobbles
Fees: $5 per day for sightseeing on Catalina Highway

Mt. Lemmon is the high point of the Santa Catalina Mountains, a rugged range on the fringe of Tucson that encompasses everything from deep gorges to rocky heights, cholla cactus to fir trees, a lake, several creeks, a small mountain community, even a ski area—the southern-most one in the United States. An encapsulated view of this diverse range can be gained with a simple hours' drive up Mt. Lemmon.

Catalina Highway, Mt. Lemmon Road, Sky Island Scenic Byway, General Hitchcock Highway; whatever you call it, this is one of America's best drives. The road was constructed with prison labor starting in 1933. Seventeen years later, the monumental task of carving a road through this craggy landscape was finally finished. General Frank Harris Hitchcock, the postmaster general during Taft's administration, provided the impetus to start the project, hence the honorary highway title. Much has been made of the route's traverse through environmental life zones that "span from Mexico to Canada." True enough, traveling from the Sonoran Desert to a conifer forest in such a short distance is remarkable, and this road has probably exposed more people to the concept of life zones than any other. Still, a drive up Mt. Lemmon is more like going from the bottom of Mt. Lemmon to the top, not quite all the way to Canada.

Veritable forests of saguaro cactus cover south facing slopes adjacent to the highway up to the 4,000' elevation before grasslands and scattered oak communities begin to dominate. By mile 10, at 5,500', the shade of upper Bear Canyon produces an uncommon forest of mature cypress trees. The first pines appear at mile 11, as the road approaches the 6,000' level. The majority are common ponderosa pines, but you might also look for the dark bark and short needles of the Chihuahua pine, a native of Mexico that stretches tentacles of its range into southern Arizona. Southern exposure at mile 12 brings a return of oaks and also pinyon pine, but the real highlight

The anticlimatic summit of Lemmon

here is geology rather than botany. Look for charismatic rocky turrets, or hoodoos, that cover the mountainside. These granitic formations are the result of weathering on the especially grainy rock, which is part of the biggest metamorphic mountain complex in the entire Basin and Range Province.

Towers atop Mt. Bigelow come into view to the northwest past mile 14. The road then straddles a ridge revealing the Rincon Mountains to the southeast. Perhaps the best roadside vista comes at mile 17.2, where a kiosk illustrates the San Pedro River Valley to the east. Past the 20 mile mark, the highway makes its first descent. Now traversing the top of the range, it winds through a forest of Douglas fir and aspen, two widespread species that do actually grow in Canada.

At 24.6 miles, the main road leads downhill toward the community of Summerhaven, but the summit of Mt. Lemmon is up the right fork past the ski valley, on road #11. It is 1.5 more miles to parking lots at the ski area, where a gate sometimes blocks the remaining 1.75 miles of road to the summit. If the gate is open, the drive continues up a pot-holed paved road to more parking at trailheads on the summit ridge. If the gate is closed, the road provides a gentle walking route to the top.

The actual high point of Mt. Lemmon is held captive behind gates at a mountaintop observatory. To stand on the very summit, you'll have to get friendly with an astronomer.

Even if you can't arrange a summit visit, a decent view can be had with just a short walk off the road on the summit ridge. If you are able to make a longer walk down an old road of loose cobbles, a much better view is found at Lemmon Rock Lookout. This is located 0.75 miles and 300 vertical feet below the trailhead parking at the top, on a signed route called the Mt. Lemmon Trail.

Access: From north central Tucson, Grant Road leads east to Tanque Verde Road. Take Tanque Verde Road to Catalina Highway, and turn north, following signs for Mt. Lemmon. A fee is charged for sightseeing along the Catalina Highway: $5 per day, $10 per week, $20 per year. Passes are available at a booth located roadside near the bottom of the mountain, or at the Sabino Canyon visitor center.

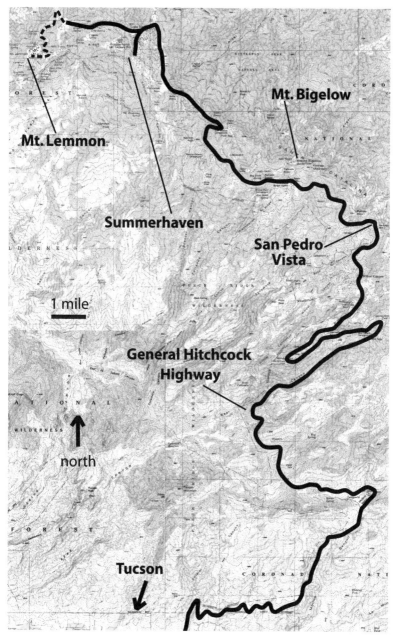

Mt. Bigelow

Mt. Lemmon

Summerhaven

San Pedro Vista

1 mile

General Hitchcock Highway

north

Tucson

| Paved Road | Dirt Road | Trail | Route |

Kitt Peak

DRIVE

General Description: A drive to the renowned Kitt Peak Observatories
Summit Elevation: 6,880'
Vertical Gain: 3,650' from Ajo Highway to the summit
Round-Trip Distance: 25 miles from the highway
Optimal Season: Anytime except Thanksgiving, Christmas, and New Years
Route Surface and Difficulty: Paved road with turnouts

For four decades, Kitt Peak has been a favorite summit of tourists and locals alike who explore from Tucson. The huge white Mayall telescope atop Kitt Peak has been a recognizable landmark in southeastern Arizona since its construction in 1970. A dozen years before the Mayall was built, the National Science Foundation selected the Tohono O'odham's (pronounced Toe ah'no O ott em) Kitt Peak as the site for a collection of telescopes. The assemblage has now grown into the largest group of high-powered telescopes in the world. Besides the noticeable Mayall, Kitt Peak boasts twenty-two other big scopes, including the McMath-Pierce telescope—the largest solar telescope in the world.

Many of the working telescopes are off-limits to the public, but several are open for viewing. Guided tours take place three times daily, and a visitor center is open from 9 a.m. to 3:45 p.m. Much of the activity on Kitt Peak begins after the grounds close at 4 p.m., when the community of astronomers who live on the summit start their day, or, night.

Whether you are a space enthusiast or not, a drive to the summit of Kitt Peak can provide a pleasant day-outing. The maintained paved road climbs the north and west sides of the peak, traversing slopes of granite above the valley floor. The big conical mountain rising to the north is Gu Achi, one of the most prominent formations on Tohono O'odham land.

Stunted, spreading mesquite trees border the road, along with showy white stalks of Sotol, a useful basket weaving plant. Thick hedges of manzanita line the roadside starting at 5,000', and a forest, predominantly of oak, covers the upper slopes of the mountain.

There are plenty of pullouts along the route offering a chance to rest and enjoy the surroundings. The largest pullouts exist at the following mile points: 7.3, 9.3, 9.9, 10.2, 10.6, 11.0, 11.3, 11.4, 11.8. A designated picnic area with tables, ramadas, and bathrooms is located north of the road about a mile below the top.

Near the summit, various nearby mountains are visible. The pinnacle of Baboquivari first comes into view at mile 8.5. The craggy Coyote Mountains

Kitt Peak Road traverses rugged slopes of the Quinlan Mountains

are just east of Kitt Peak, viewable from several locations at the summit area. In a peculiar twist of nomenclature, the Coyote Mountains are one of three named mountain groups that make up the Baboquivari Range. Kitt Peak is part of the Quinlan Mountains, while farther south the mountains are simply called the Baboquivaris. All three named ranges are born of the same geology—a single metamorphic core complex typical of the Basin and Range Province.

Although no one location is optimal for a sweeping 360° view, vantage points in all four directions can be found with short walks from the visitor center. The true summit of Kitt Peak is north of the visitor center, at the base of the giant Mayall telescope. If you've gone this far, you might as well take the elevator up the telescope, then follow stairs to an enclosed circular viewing room. This is probably Kitt Peak's best lookout, for terrestrial formations anyway.

Access: From Tucson, head west on Highway 86—Ajo Highway—about 35 miles to milepost 135.2. This is about 15 miles past Robles Junction, also known as Three Points. Follow signs south off the highway to Kitt Peak. The summit road leads 12.3 miles from the highway to a visitor center parking area.

Babo from Kitt

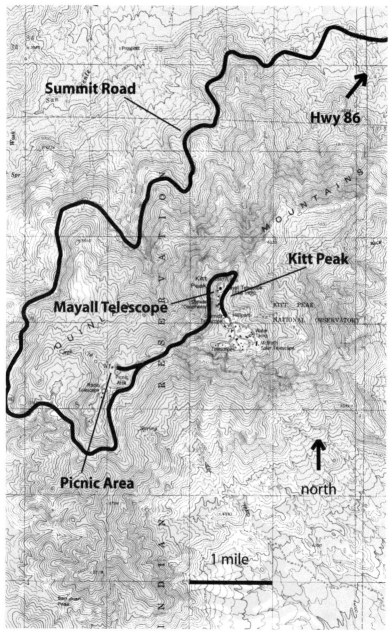

Summit Road

Hwy 86

Kitt Peak

Mayall Telescope

Picnic Area

↑ north

1 mile

Paved Road	Dirt Road	Trail	Route

Harquahala Mountain

DRIVE

General Description: A four-wheel-drive road to a prominent Arizona summit with remarkable history
Summit Elevation: 5,681'
Vertical Gain: 3,868'
Round-Trip Distance: 21 miles from Eagle Eye Road to summit and back
Optimal Season: April — November / Anytime the road isn't wet from snow or rain
Route Surface and Difficulty: Rocky road with sharp loose cobbles, bedrock ledges, and steep hills

"Ah qua hala" is what native people called this mountain, meaning "there is water, high up." When settlers arrived, minerals on the mountain were of chief interest, and mining activity is what gave birth to the road that now leads to the top. The route is a designated backcountry byway, with informational kiosks located both at the summit and the base of the mountain.

The base kiosk comes just a few hundred yards from paved Eagle Eye Road. Beyond this, the road strikes out across gentle desert slopes of alluvium for about 3 miles before merging into Blue Tank Canyon. The road surface degenerates a notch once in the canyon, although a mellow grade keeps the route relatively passable.

The first steep hill comes 4 miles from pavement, where the Monterrey Mine jeep trail forks to the right. It's another mile of steady traversing up the canyon until the first big climb, and hence four-wheel-drive conditions. After a couple steep switchback turns over ledgy bedrock, the road crests a ridge at 3,150', and long views of distant landforms open to the southwest. The route continues following the ridge, climbing a loose, steep, and rocky corner in another quarter-mile. Another steep climb, this one straddling the ridgeline, comes at just over 7 miles from the bottom.

As the views get bigger, the route gets more challenging. Steep pitches strewn with sharp oil-pan-skewering boulders come at miles 9.0 and 9.2. Just past this sustained "nine-mile-hill" comes a reprieve, where concrete has been poured on the road to prevent erosion. Once reaching the concrete, you've passed the crux, but it's still another mile to the top.

The summit area served as home and scientific research base in the early 1920s, and several kiosks tell the story. Harquahala Mountain was selected by the Smithsonian Astrophysical Observatory as an ideal location to measure sun rays in testing Dr. Samual Langley's solar constant theory. His protege Dr. Charles Abbott picked up the research, and assigned Alfred

Alfred and Chella's front yard view

Moore and his wife Chella to live at Harquahala. The backcountry byway of today was barely a horse trail back then, so everything had to be hauled to the summit via a mule trail on the north side of the mountain.

Once settled in, the scientists began their experiments through mind-boggling procedure. The sun shone on a coelostat, while its heat triggered a pyranometer, and its rays registered on the pyrheliometer. After that, it was a simple process of reading the spectrometer-bolometer on the galvanometer, which reflected onto the bolograph. Next came a little math, and bam-zoom, they were done.

The observatory was moved to a mountain top in California by the mid-twenties, but the house/research lab building remains as a historical feature. The homestead might have been low on amenities, but it was great on views.

In the southeast, the Sierra Estrella Mountains poke above Phoenix haze, which creeps westerly across valleys punctuated by ranges like the nearby Big Horns. Looking southeast beyond Big Horn Peak, a cloud often floats above the Palo Verde Nuclear Facility. West of this, the dome of Woolsey Peak floats on the lower atmosphere. Craggy tail feathers of Eagle Tail Peak are visible to the south across Interstate 10 and the Harquahala Plain. Castle Dome Peak presents a perky nipple on the horizon in the far southwest, and the sawtoothed Kofa Mountains rise farther north. To the distant northwest is Crossman Mountain near Lake Havasu, and the Hualapai Range near Kingman. The Aquarius and Mohon Mountains capture the northern horizon, and lonely Mt. Hope stands butte-like in the flat expanse near the headwaters of Burro Creek. In winter, the Bradshaw Mountains are often snow covered in the northeast, as are the Mazatzals in the far east-northeast. That range's southern component, the Four Peaks, are visible on good days, 110 miles to the east, rising beyond Phoenix.

There is a hiking route to the top of Harquahala Mountain as well. This is the route used by the summit residents and researchers in the 1920s. The trail is 5.4 miles long, gains 3,360', and is maintained. The trailhead is located on the north side of the mountain, 2.1 miles down a dirt road off Highway 60. Turn between mileposts 70 and 71, across from a palm tree.

Access: From Phoenix, take I-10 west about 50 miles to exit #81 for Salome Road. Take Salome Road northwest for 9.6 miles to Eagle Eye Road. Follow Eagle Eye Road north for 8.5 miles to the Harquahala Mountain Backcountry Byway.

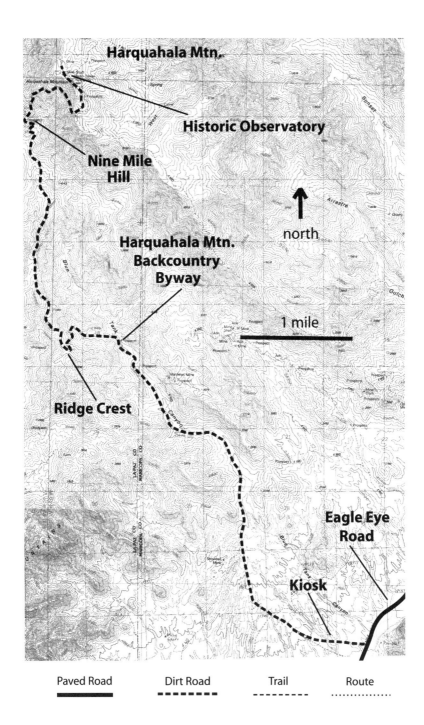

Harquahala Mtn.

Historic Observatory

Nine Mile Hill

Harquahala Mtn. Backcountry Byway

north

1 mile

Ridge Crest

Eagle Eye Road

Kiosk

| Paved Road | Dirt Road | Trail | Route |

HIKES

Piestewa Peak

HIKE

General Description: A trail hike up a striking peak surrounded by city
Summit Elevation: 2,608'
Vertical Gain: 1,304'
Round-Trip Distance: 3 miles
Optimal Season: November — March, early mornings from spring through autumn
Route Surface and Difficulty: Maintained trail with heavy hiker traffic

Like Camelback Mountain, Piestewa Peak is a desert island amidst the urban sea of greater Phoenix. Of the two, however, Piestewa Peak has a more dramatic summit, and because of its location within the Phoenix Mountains Preserve, it offers more extended hiking options than Camelback.

Piestewa Peak's craggy drama results from its geology. The mountain is composed primarily of schist, an ancient metamorphic rock that forms angular knife-edge ridges and fins. Much of the Piestewa Peak Trail is constructed out of this schist, stacked meticulously in a solid rock stairway leading to the top of the mountain.

The summit trail begins as a concrete walkway that switchbacks up the east face of the mountain. Once gaining the southwest ridge, the route more or less follows the ridgeline all the way to the summit. Along the way, the trail crosses the ridge divide a couple times, traversing slopes that rise above downtown Phoenix to the west. There are a couple steep spots where hikers must negotiate short ledges made of the peak's trademark gray bedrock. The steepest of these ledge-steps comes just below the top, a fitting climax to this popular hill climb.

The final steep pitch occupies a narrow depression, making hikers share a confined area that is indicative of Piestewa Peak. Almost the entire Piestewa Peak Trail is hacked into a hard rocky mountainside, so the path is much narrower than Camelback Mountain's wider route.

Many Piestewa Peak hikers enjoy the summit view from an area that is readily apparent to the left of the trail. True high pointers will notice that the actual summit is a narrow fin of schist located about 100 feet to the east of the more popular "summit" area. There is some real exposure off the east edge of the true summit, and a good view into the heart of the Phoenix Mountains Preserve.

Many long time Valley residents knew the name of this mountain as Squaw Peak, its original title. The mountain was re-named in 2004 after

Benchmark and hikers atop Piestewa Peak

Arizona's Lori Piestewa, who was killed in action serving in Iraq. Lori was from Tuba City, AZ, where she grew up as a member of the Hopi tribe. She was the first Native American woman to die as a result of combat.

Access: From Phoenix, take Freeway 51 to Lincoln Drive, and head east about a half mile to Squaw Peak Drive. Turn left on Squaw Peak Drive and follow it through a residential neighborhood to one of the many parking areas in this part of the Phoenix Mountains Preserve. The first lot on the left is closest to the summit trailhead, but with a short walk, any of the lots offer access to the Summit Trail.

Piestewa Peak Trail

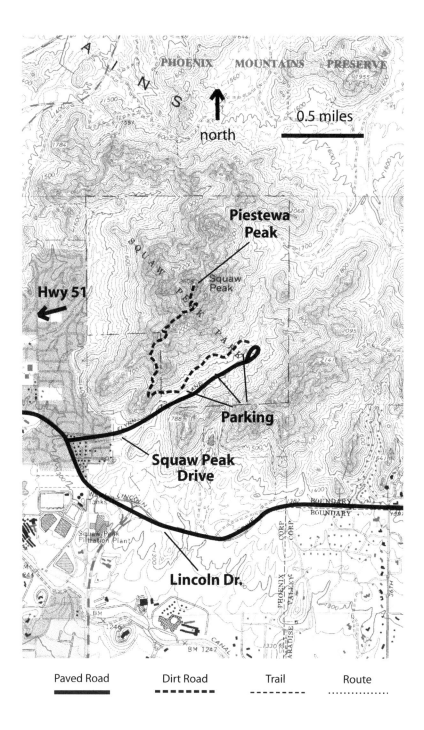

PHOENIX MOUNTAINS PRESERVE

↑ north

0.5 miles

Piestewa Peak

Squaw Peak

Hwy 51 ←

Parking

Squaw Peak Drive

Lincoln Dr.

| Paved Road | Dirt Road | Trail | Route |

Chiricahua Crest

HIKE

General Description: A long day hike or backpack along the spine of the Chiricahua Mountains
Summit Elevations: Flys Peak—9,667' / Chiricahua Peak—9,759' / Paint Rock—9,375' / Monte Vista Peak—9,373'
Vertical Gain: 1,359' from Rustler Park to Chiricahua Peak / About 2,500' total gain along entire crest route
Round-trip Distance: 10 miles to Chiricahua Peak / 16 miles round-trip to Monte Vista Peak via the ridge trail
Optimal Season: late April — November / Snow closes Chiricahua trails and roads in winter.
Route Surface and Difficulty: Trail with occasional deadfall / off-trail open forest

There are a number of trails in the Chiricahua Mountains, many of which have degenerated in recent years. When hiking here, expect to detour around fallen logs, and hack through encroaching brush. One trail that is still relatively intact is the popular Chiricahua Ridge Trail that starts at the north end of Rustler Park Campground.

The Ridge Trail climbs above the campground, then traverses the east side of the range crest en route to Bootlegger Saddle, about 2 miles distant. The trail climbs burned slopes beyond Bootlegger Saddle, then descends to another saddle called Flys Park.

From Flys Park, it is possible to loop back to the campground by hiking a trail to road #42D which leads to Rustler Park Campground. When road #42D is open to vehicles, it is possible to start hiking from its end, and cut about 2 miles off the route to Chiricahua and Monte Vista Peaks.

At Flys Park, the ridge trail crosses to the western slopes of the range, circumventing Flys Peak. To summit Flys Peak, continue straight from the Flys Park/saddle on a vague unmaintained trail that leads to the top. There is an ancient windblown forest on the 9,667' summit, with good views to the west. By descending the burned southern slope of Flys Peak, you will reach Round Park (another meadowed saddle), where you can re-join the ridge trail.

Continuing south, the trail cuts a nice flat traverse around an unnamed hill to Cima Park, then climbs steadily across steep forested slopes to Junction Saddle at the base of Chiricahua Peak.

At 9,759', Chiricahua Peak is the high point of the range, but its summit is covered in forest, offering only glimpses of the surrounding country. You

See forever from the Chiricahua Crest

can reach the peak by ascending directly up a ridge from Junction Saddle. To re-join the ridge trail from the summit, the surest route is a backtrack to Junction Saddle. If you hate backtracking, and are comfortable with route finding in steep dense forest, you might enter thick forests on the peak's southwest ridge, and descend to the Aspen Saddle Trail, then head west to the ridge trail. If you are in search of big views, and not so interested in the forested high point of Chiricahua Peak, you can avoid the peak altogether, and follow the ridge on a gradual mile-long descent from Junction Saddle to Chiricahua Saddle.

From Chiricahua Saddle, the trail follows the east side of the range divide, with intriguing views into rugged Rucker Canyon. After meandering past Paint Rock and a few other outcrops, it veers west into the forests on Raspberry Peak. There is one last trail junction before a short uphill climb to the summit of Monte Vista Peak at 9,373', where there is a cabin, a lookout tower, and a spectacular view.

A runner could make it to Monte Vista Peak and back to Rustler Park Campground in a day, but for most this is an overnight excursion. There are several springs near the route, and good bivouac spots along the way.

Access: Take Routes 186 and 181 toward Chiricahua National Monument, and turn right onto Pinery Canyon Road #42 at milepost 64. Follow this gravel, then dirt, then rocky road up Pinery Canyon into the mountains. At 13.5 miles past the pavement, turn right onto road #420 at Onion Saddle. Road #420 beyond Onion Saddle will give low clearance cars difficulty. It's steep and rocky. In a little over 2 miles from the saddle, stay left at a fork toward Rustler Park, which is less than a mile farther.

When road #42D is open, it is possible to continue past Rustler Park to the end of #42D, and join the ridge trail at Flys Park.

Aspen trees of the Chiricahua Sky Island

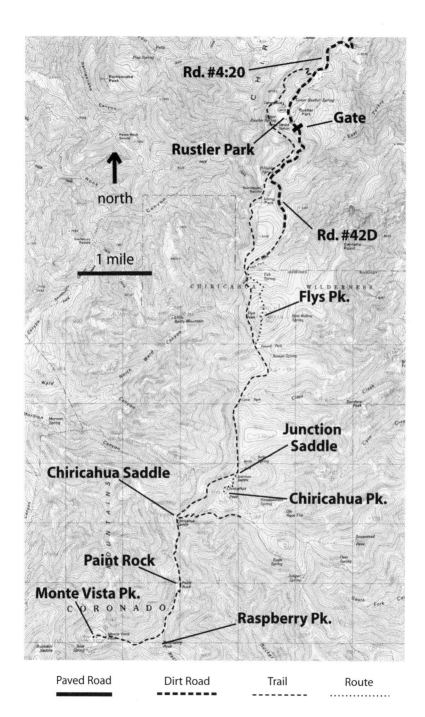

Rd. #4:20

Gate

Rustler Park

Rd. #42D

north

1 mile

Flys Pk.

Junction Saddle

Chiricahua Saddle

Chiricahua Pk.

Paint Rock

Monte Vista Pk.

Raspberry Pk.

| Paved Road | Dirt Road | Trail | Route |

Mt. Wrightson

HIKE

General Description: A well maintained trail to a high treeless summit
Summit Elevation: 9,453'
Vertical Gain: 3,933'
Round-Trip Distance: 10.4 miles
Optimal Season: March — November / Watch out for lightning during monsoon season
Route Surface and Difficulty: Maintained trail

Attention view hounds! The summit of Mt. Wrightson offers the best single viewpoint in southern Arizona. The narrow barren summit is higher than anything for miles, and a 360° overlook is the result.

Immediately across the Santa Cruz River to the southwest are the craggy blue Tumacacori Mountains. Mt. Hopkins and its giant observatory sits in the immediate foreground. To the west is the dramatic shark tooth of Baboquivari, and at the north end of that range, the white buildings of Kitt Peak observatory. The Santa Catalinas and Rincons are not far to the north, above the city of Tucson. Beyond Rincon Peak to the northeast are the Pinaleno Mountains, home to Mt. Graham and Heliograph Peak. With binoculars, you might be able to pick out the twin bumps of Dos Cabezas on the next mountain horizon eastward. Four small distinct humps identify the Chiricahua Mountains, located three ranges to the east of Wrightson. Continuing southwest, there are the Mule Mountains near Bisbee, and the nearby Huachucas. Many landmarks of Sonora, Mexico can also be seen. The smog of Nogales hovers in the valley on the southern U.S. border, with a string of development running from there along the Santa Cruz River, past the foot of Mt. Wrightson, all the way to Tucson.

To reach this fabulous viewpoint, one can pick from several good trails. The most popular and direct is the Old Baldy Trail, starting from the highest parking lot in the Madera Canyon Recreation Area.

The Old Baldy begins as a closed dirt road, but soon narrows into a broad foot path as it traverses north and east facing slopes along the upper middle fork of Madera Canyon. The ascent is relatively gradual, but unrelenting. Various oaks, and Apache and Chiricahua pines provide spotty shade.

A little over 2 miles of steady uphill walking will bring you to Josephine Saddle, a major intersection of the Santa Rita Mountains. From here, the Agua Caliente Trail heads east, the Josephine Canyon Trail drops southward, and the Super Trail leads north on the opposite side of the drainage you've been following. The summit-bound Old Baldy Trail continues its gradual

Looking north down the spine of the Santa Ritas from Mt. Wrightson

climb with a long traverse across the western slopes of the mountain.

After passing Bellows Spring, the trail makes tight switchbacks between rock buttresses to Baldy Saddle. The final 700 vertical feet is another series of switchbacks leading up the northeast side of the peak. The trail finally breaks out of the forest for the final strides to southern Arizona's best viewpoint.

Access: From I-19 about 30 miles south of Tucson, take exit #63 at Continental Road. Head east on Continental Road about 1 mile, crossing the Santa Cruz River before turning right on Whitehouse Canyon Road. Follow the signs from here to Madera Canyon Recreation Area. It is about 13 miles from the Whitehouse Canyon turn to the parking lot at the base of the Old Baldy Trail.

Nearby Mt. Hopkins and its observatory

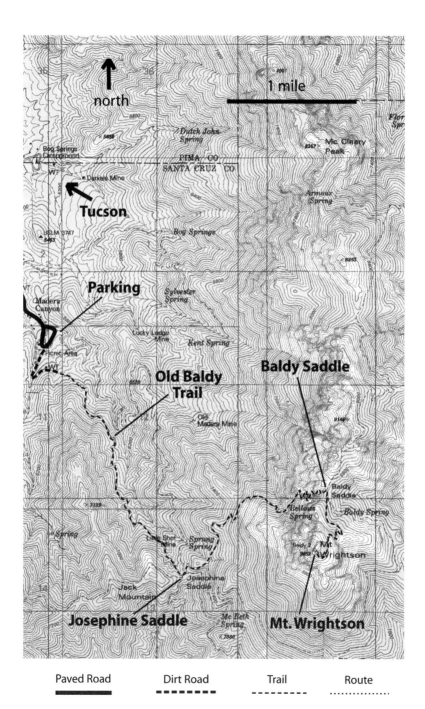

north

1 mile

Tucson

Parking

Baldy Saddle

Old Baldy
Trail

Josephine Saddle

Mt. Wrightson

Paved Road	Dirt Road	Trail	Route

Signal Peak

HIKE

General Description: A convoluted route to the high point of the Kofa Mountains
Summit Elevation: 4,877'
Vertical Gain: 2,037'
Round-Trip Distance: 6 miles
Optimal Season: November — March
Route Surface and Difficulty: Rudimentary trail / off-trail desert with occasional moderate brush

The Kofa Mountains are an exceptionally vertical and craggy desert range in southwestern Arizona. Named for the cattle brand (K of A) of the King of Arizona Ranch, the range is the centerpiece for the Kofa National Wildlife Refuge, established in 1939 primarily for the protection of desert bighorn sheep.

The high point of the Kofa Mountains is Signal Peak, located on the western margin of the range. Contrary to the character of the Kofas, Signal Peak consists of a broad and gentle summit. Still, getting there requires a winding route through a jumbled Kofa landscape. Some might be discouraged by the elusive nature of this hidden mountain top, but the varied and circuitous route leading to Signal Peak undeniably gives this route a unique charm.

From the road in Kofa Queen Canyon, an intermittent trail leads up the cobble creekbed of Ten Ewe and Indian Canyons, heading straight for Ten Ewe Mountain. This route / trail is apparent for much of the way up Signal Peak, but it does splinter and vanish at times. To locate it for the first hill climb, veer slightly left (south) as Indian Canyon wash bends right (southwest) at the base of the mountain.

The trail ascends a slope before merging with a ridge opposite a prominent cave. The ridge is blocked by rocky outcrops above here, so the route feeds into a brushy draw and leads to a craggy saddle at 3,850'.

From this first saddle, it is best to traverse left to Ten Ewe saddle below the western cliffs of Ten Ewe Mountain, rather than descending into the basin of upper Indian Canyon. At the Ten Ewe saddle, a stunning view opens to the south, looking across the King Valley to Castle Dome Peak. The route briefly follows the spine of the Kofas from here, climbing west / southwest over a knoll to a pass at the very head of Indian Canyon. There are different options for reaching the summit from here. The easiest and most direct route continues west a hundred yards into a drainage that then leads up to open

Signal Peak's summit ridge and the rugged Kofas

slopes where the summit of Signal Peak is finally visible. At this point the lure of the top will carry you the final few hundred feet to your goal.

Yuma is visible to the southwest. The distant Hualapai Mountains can be seen to the north, recognized by an unnatural looking notch on their skyline. Harquahala Mountain is dominant in the middle distance to the northeast, with the Bradshaw Mountains looming over its right shoulder. Continuing east and southeast, other Arizona summits are visible, including Big Horn Peak, Eagle Tail Peak, and Woolsey Peak.

Access: From Quartzite, take Highway 95 south about 19 miles to mile 85.5, and turn east onto signed Palm Canyon Road. This gravel road leads 6.4 miles to the Kofa National Wildlife Refuge boundary and kiosk. Turn left here onto Kofa Queen Canyon Road, and follow it north, then east toward the mountains. At 0.8 miles from Palm Canyon Road, there is a jeep track forking left. Stay right on the more major Kofa Queen Canyon Road. Nearly 5 miles in, the road passes a campsite at a rock pinnacle, and drops left into Kofa Queen Canyon Wash. Naturally, the road gets rougher, weeding out most non four-wheel-drives. The road weaves a braided course up the bouldery wash, splitting into parallel tracks more than once. At 2.8 slow miles after entering the streambed, the road passes Ten Ewe Canyon Wash on the south. There is often a cairn here indicating the Signal Peak route. This is 7.7 miles from Palm Canyon Road. Coordinates for the start of the route are: N33°22.106' / W114°03.691'

Signal Peak—a remarkably mellow summit route amid the craggy Kofa Mountians

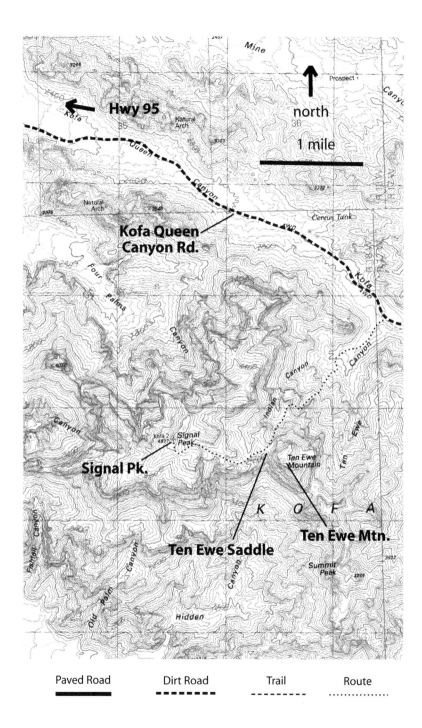

Rincon Peak

HIKE

General Description: A long trail in the Rincon Mountains
Summit Elevation: 8,482'
Vertical Gain: 4,288'
Round Trip Distance: 15 miles
Optimal Season: April — November
Route Surface and Difficulty: Trail / steep trail with some steep loose sections

Rincon Peak is not the high point of the Rincon Mountains. That honor goes to Mica Mountain, a broad blob of a peak covered in thick forest and lacking any summit view. Rincon Peak, on the other hand, casts a striking shape on the southern flank of the range, and it is only 182 feet lower than Mica Mountain. The summit of Rincon Peak is rocky and windswept, with views stretching into Mexico. For quality peak bagging in the Rincons, this is the place to go.

There are several approaches to the peak via trails within Saguaro National Park. Most of these trails are too long to complete in a single day, and a backcountry permit is required to camp overnight in the park. If you have the time, a two or three day route leading to Rincon Peak would be a beautiful way to see the Rincon Mountains. The shortest trail to the summit is the Miller Creek Trail described here. This one is do-able in a single day for strong hikers.

Not too ironically, the Miller Creek Trail begins by following Miller Creek. For the first mile, the trail curves beneath mature oaks, and crosses the intermittent stream a few times. At 1.5 miles, the park boundary is crossed, and the trail starts to climb.

For the next few miles, it winds around large granite boulders and through a thick blanket of manzanita, oak, and juniper, among other chaparral species. Classic Southeastern Arizona views open to the east, with rolling grasslands leading to linear blue ranges.

As the trail nears the crest of the range, it traverses a north facing slope in a small canyon, and the surroundings change abruptly. A dense forest of mostly white and silverleaf oaks mingles with Chihuahua and ponderosa pines.

Soon after the change of scenery, the Rincon Divide is reached. A major trail junction offers access to other parts of the range from here. The trail toward the peak leads into Happy Valley Saddle, a gorgeous basin that is home to a backcountry campground and some impressive old pine trees. If

On the trail to Rincon

you are planning a two day assault on Rincon Peak, this is a great place for a base camp.

Just as the trail seems to be heading down the basin and away from the peak, it veers south and again begins to climb the slopes of the Rincons. In this sun and wind hammered zone, the tall trees of the basin are replaced by a stunted forest of pinyon pines and junipers. The trail continues the ascent via some switchbacks and long traverses between drainages. Views occasionally open westward to the Santa Cruz Valley, and Rincon Peak pokes out from beyond forested ridges.

For the final summit push, the trail steepens significantly. There are a couple boulder steps, and some short slopes of ball-bearing gravels. The surrounding forest opens as pines and firs soar overhead. Curving to the south side of the peak, the trail once again enters chaparral before busting onto the open rocky summit.

A massive rock monument sits on the high point, adorned with a creative prayer flag constructed from selected garments of local peak maidens.

Access: From Tucson, take I-10 east about 30 miles to exit #297. Head north on Mescal Road. The road turns to dirt in 3 miles. It is generally a decent maintained road, but it does cross a few streambeds that can present challenges for city cars. After one of these wash crossings 14.7 miles from the freeway, turn left at a sign for the Miller Creek Trailhead. This turn is just beyond a ranch pasture. After the left turn, proceed about 70 yards and turn left again at a big oak tree. It is another 150 yards to the trailhead.

Southeast morning

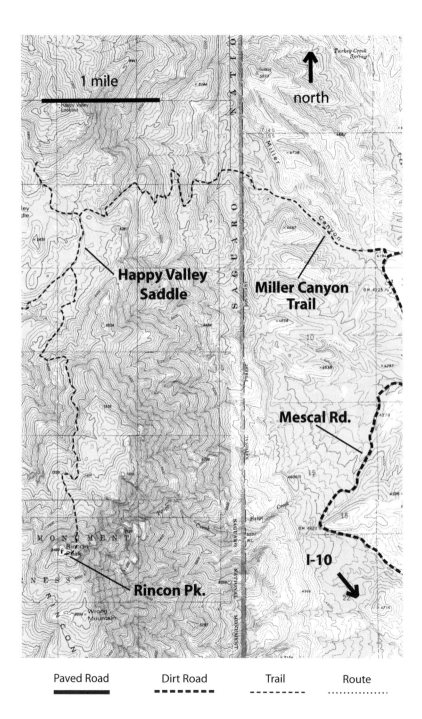

Cochise Head

HIKE

General Description: A remote summit with an interesting approach
Summit Elevation: 8,113'
Vertical Gain: 2,200'
Round-Trip Distance: 9 miles
Optimal Season: March — April, October — November
Route Surface and Difficulty: Dirt road / narrow trail / cairned route on steep loose dirt

Cochise Head is a spectacular formation of tuff in the northern Chiricahua Mountains. Guarded by a miasma of rugged mountains carpeted with chaparral, Cochise Head resides in fierce country worthy of the peak's namesake Apache leader. There are no outfitted trailheads or groomed esplanades leading to this summit. That, of course, is part of the attraction.

On my first visit here, I arrived expecting a cross country bushwhack approach. After hacking past head high staghorn cholla, and trying to decipher my map position in complex terrain, I came across a trail. It wasn't really going my direction, but it was better than the hack-fest I was engaged in, so I followed it. Before long, the trail began bending towards Cochise Head, and I soon realized that my bushwhacking foray was over. Hallelujah.

There are a few different approaches one can take to reach Cochise Head. The one described here has the advantages of an easy drive and the shortest hiking distance. It does, however, descend a few hundred feet to a low pass before climbing to the peak. The varied terrain requires some extra effort, but it also adds to the adventure, and ultimately, to the appeal of the route.

Near the parking spot in Bonita Park, there is a gated service road that offers easy access through a thick pygmy forest. Follow this dirt road about a mile to the abandoned King of Lead Mine, and hold your breath against the stinky emanations that seem to linger at this old dig spot. Soon after passing the mine, the road crests the first of two ridges. At the second ridge about a quarter-mile past the mine, a grassy saddle surrounds the ruins of an old horse camp, and the road diminishes. Look for cairns on the left here. For GPS navigators, the coordinates at this junction are: N32°.02.458' W109°.18.348'.

The cairns are signalling the "Horse Trail," a narrow path that traverses into Indian Creek Canyon. The trail gently climbs before crossing a finger ridge, and then makes a gradual 1-mile descent to a pass between Indian Creek and Wood Canyons. At the pass there are old trail signs, one of which indicates the route to Cochise Head.

Cochise Head of the northern Chiricahuas

The trail to the Head is vague, and hard to find at times. Basically it heads up the ridge connecting the Indian Creek / Wood Canyon pass to the Head. There are cairns along portions of the route, but in many places there are none at all. There is no definitive single route, but all paths tend to gravitate to the ridge. Keep your eyes open, travel with confidence, and don't stray too far from the ridge.

Once at the lichened cliffs guarding the western flank of the peak, the route contours around to the shady north side, and becomes slightly more discernible as it leads through oak groves and across talus slopes. Don't get lured uphill too soon near the top. The best route continues to contour until reaching a majestic windswept saddle between Cochise Head and its eastern hump. From here, an easy slope through scattered chaparral leads to the summit.

The view is spectacular from the top. The Chiricahuas fill the southern horizon, with fluted tuff pinnacles decorating plateau edges in the foreground. Mexico's Sierra San Jose is a classically shaped A-frame peak in the southwest. The Huachuca Mountains form the skyline westward of this. Across the sweeping grasslands and scattered irrigation patterns of the Sulphur Springs Valley sit the Dragoon Mountains. North of them is the nipple of Rincon Peak, and the dome of Mica Mountain. The next blue dome northward is the Santa Catalina Range. The twin heads of Dos Cabezas are not far to the west of Cochise Head. The high sloping Pinalenos are to the right of Dos Cabezas. Circular irrigation of the San Simon Valley is apparent to the north, with the low Peloncillo Mountains beyond the valley. This disjunct range runs in an arc from here all the way to the border with Mexico. In New Mexico, there are many other ranges within view, including the Mogollon Mountains in the distant northeast, and the Big Hatchet Mountains in the southeast. This range appears as four ascending humps on the horizon, just to the right of Cochise Head's eastern hump.

Access: From Willcox, take Route 186 southeast for about 30 miles, and head east on Route 181 to Chiricahua National Monument. Enter the monument ($5 entrance fee in 2009) and continue past the visitor center, following the main road up Bonita Canyon.

At 3.5 miles past the visitor center, there is a small gravel parking shoulder on the north side of the road that can serve as the start of the route. This is located after the road has entered Bonita Park above the canyon, but before it begins to steeply climb around the mountain toward Sugarloaf Mountain Trailhead. There is another wide shoulder with an ancient streambeds kiosk about 150 yards beyond the gravel shoulder.

About 150 yards down the road from the gravel parking shoulder, there is a gated service road that offers easy walking toward the King of Lead Mine, and eventually, Cochise Head.

There is no camping allowed at the trailhead, but there is a national monument campground in lower Bonita Canyon. There is also good camping in Pinery Canyon along road #42, a few miles from the monument entrance.

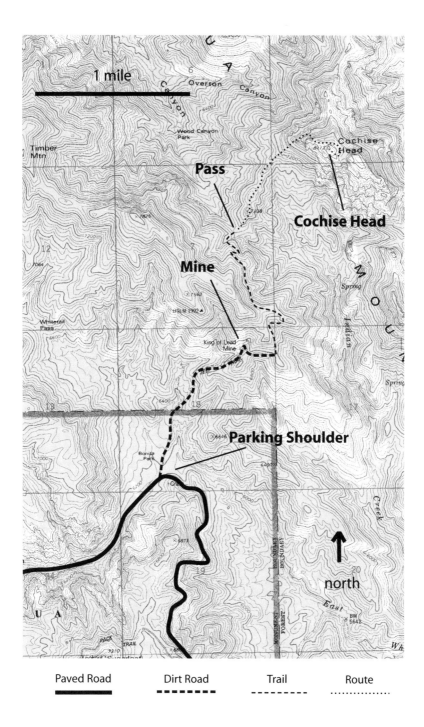

1 mile

Timber Mtn

Overton Canyon

Wood Canyon Park

Pass

Cochise Head

Cochise Head

Mine

Whitetail Pass

King of Lead Mine

Spring

Parking Shoulder

Bonita Park

Creek

north

BM 5642

| Paved Road | Dirt Road | Trail | Route |

Bassett Peak

HIKE

General Description: A trail hike through forest and along open ridges
Summit Elevation: 7,663'
Vertical Gain: 2,750'
Round-Trip Distance: 12 miles
Optimal Season: October — November, March — April
Route Surface and Difficulty: ATV track / foot path / use-trail through light brush

The Galiuro Mountains are a rugged range of unusual tuff (volcanic ash deposits) formations. Several high points along the spine of the range breach the 7,000' mark, and Basset Peak is the highest of these promontories. The slopes of the relatively remote Galiuros are covered in dense brush, while the canyon bottoms support pleasant shady forests.

One of these canyon forests shades the trail for the first half of the route to Basset Peak's summit. Ash Creek Road diminishes into an ATV track which doubles as a smooth foot trail for the first few miles of the route. Leading through a beautiful forest of oak (several varieties), pine (four species), fir (two types), cypress, and maple. The route crosses the normally dry creekbed a few times, and splits into parallel trails for brief periods, but it is generally easy to follow.

The Galiuro Wilderness boundary is indicated just before the trail veers west up the Ash Spring arm of the canyon. The trail steepens slightly here, following the south side of the drainage. When white-barked aspen trees appear, the trail crosses the creekbed at Ash Spring, and begins a 700-foot climb to the ridge above. GPS coordinates for this important change of course are: N32°.30.997' W110°.16.509'.

The foot trail becomes rockier as it makes a gradual but steady climb past scenic fins of tuff and stunted pines. There is one section of switchbacks just before reaching the range divide about 4 miles from the trailhead.

Continuing south on the crest trail, the route mostly stays on the west side of the divide. Great views of the Galiuro's colorful lichened rocks adorn the ridge walk. One final set of switchbacks leads up the shady forested north face of Bassett Peak.

When the trail tops out at 7,500' just west of the peak, two options remain for reaching the summit. Steeper use trails head directly to the top from here, leading through light brush en route. A slightly less steep route begins 150 yards farther down the crest trail, just short of the next ridge. This summit bound trail leads through stunted pinyon pines and junipers to the peak.

Walking in the timeless Galiuros

The summit of Bassett Peak has long been a sacred locale. Pot sherds are scattered in the area, probable remnants of mountaintop ceremonies from centuries ago. More recent history is recorded in the ramshackle summit register. One entry tells of "Papa" Bull, the rancher who rode his horse up the mountain to transport deceased airmen back down after their airplane crashed into the slopes of the peak. The wreckage is still visible from the trail, perched on a buttress on the western slopes of the mountain.

Trees are stunted enough on top to allow a wonderful 360° view. The Pinaleno Mountains dominate to the east. The little heads of Dos Cabezas poke out in the southeast. Closer are the Winchester Mountains, with the Chiricahuas in the distance behind. The southern horizon holds Sierra San Jose of Mexico, with AZ's Huachuca Mountains visible as the next range west. With binoculars, you might spot the eye in the sky blimp hovering over that range. Across the San Pedro River Valley to the west are the Rincon Mountains, with the Santa Rita's Mt. Wrightson lingering through a gap in the distance. The shark's tooth of Baboquivari cuts the skyline in the far west. Towers are vaguely visible in the nearby Santa Catalinas. Looking north, the rugged Galiuros lead the eye to the Pinal Mountains, and farther northeast, the buttressed Sierra Anchas. The highest horizon in the northeast, with a shallow v-notch, indicates the White Mountains.

Access: From Tucson, take I-10 east to Willcox and exit #340. Follow Fort Grant Road north and west about 18 miles (Ft. Grant Rd. changes to Brookerson Rd.), and follow the pavement left (west) onto Ash Creek Road. In 3 more miles, you'll arrive at the Ash Creek Road / Ft. Grant Road intersection near a cluster of grain silos: N32°28.255' W109°58.683'.

Here, Ash Creek Road turns to dirt. Follow it west, north, and west again, passing Rainbird Ranch in 11 miles, and bearing right on the main road in 13 miles. At 14.5 miles from the silo intersection, turn west into the national forest on an unmarked road (N32°30.605' W110°12.041'), as the main road continues north to become Sunset Loop. Continue past several campsites among oaks, bearing right in 0.7 miles at the road #659 junction. Proceed through a gate in another quarter-mile, and continue down the narrow but passable road about another mile. The last good parking is located at: N32°30.438' W110°14.108', just before a rough creek crossing.

From Safford, take Highway 191 south for 17 miles to Highway 266. Follow 266 west for 20 miles and take Ft. Grant Road south for 5.7 miles to the Ash Creek Road junction near a cluster of grain silos. From here, follow above directions.

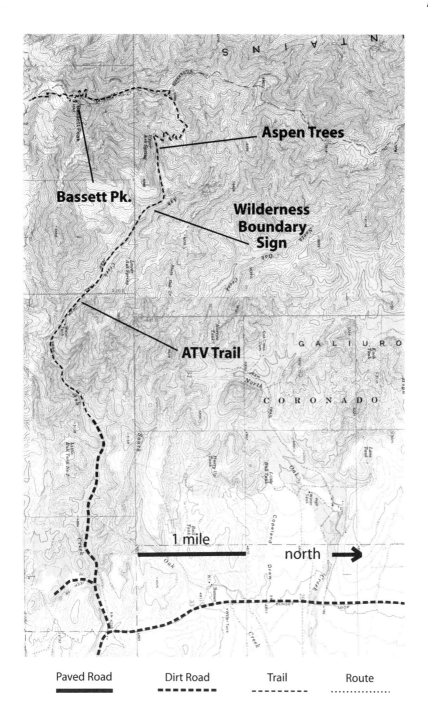

Aspen Trees

Bassett Pk.

Wilderness
Boundary
Sign

ATV Trail

1 mile

north

Paved Road   Dirt Road   Trail   Route

Miller Peak

HIKE

General Description: A trail hike to an open summit
Summit Elevation: 9,466'
Vertical Gain: 2,880'
Round-Trip Distance: 9 miles
Optimal Season: late September — November, April — June
Route Surface and Difficulty: Narrow mostly smooth trail with a few fallen boulders

Miller Peak is the high point of the Huachuca Mountains. It rises over vast grasslands of northern Mexico, just a few short miles from the international border. Due to this close proximity, the trail up Miller Peak is used perhaps as much by border crossers seeking a life in the United States as it is by peak baggers seeking the summit of the Huachucas. Scattered along the entire route are discarded water jugs, torn Chinese made day packs, random socks, empty juice cans, tuna tins, and the occasional abandoned shoe.

The route begins across the road from the Montezuma Pass parking area. The first couple miles are the steepest, as the trail struggles to maintain a moderate grade while ascending perilously steep slopes of slippery grass and daggered agaves. A few mine shafts are passed before the trail crests a breezy ridge at 7,800', where a view unfolds to the east.

Beyond the crest, dense chaparral borders the path, which cuts a mellow contour on the east side of the Huachuca's range divide. About 3.5 miles from the road, the trail crosses to the generally more sheltered west side of the divide at 8,400'. Below, a cloak of forest carpets Copper and Oversite Canyons before relenting to valley grasslands at the foot of the mountains.

At 8,600', the trail reaches a pass boasting the greatest collection of discarded equipment along the route. The reason for the trash heap seems to stem from an intersection of trails here, leading both east and west. The route to the summit continues north through pine and fir forests, and past rocky outcrops on the southwest slopes of Miller Peak.

A final intersection is reached at just over 9,000', when the Huachuca Crest Trail veers northwest, while the Miller Peak Trail climbs east via switchbacks toward the summit. This last half-mile tends to drag on as it climbs the peak's shady northwest face through white pines and aspens.

The top once held a lookout tower that has been removed. Today, a concrete slab remains. The view is open and broad. To the south are the huge plains of Mexico's San Pedro Valley. The grassland stretches in a nearly unbroken arc to the west, blending with the San Rafael Valley—headwaters

Oaks and grasslands near the Mexican border below Miller Peak

of the Santa Cruz River. The Patagonia Mountains are on the far side of the San Rafael Valley, with the Tumacacori Mountains beyond them, slightly to the north. The unmistakable Baboquivari sits in the distance, while Mt. Hopkins and Wrightson of the Santa Rita Mountains are closer in the northwest. The twin domes of the Santa Catalinas and the Rincons are almost due north, with the lower Whetstone Mountains sitting at their feet. As the eye pans northeastward, Ft. Huachuca's surveillance blimp disturbs the scene, hovering over the sprawl of Sierra Vista. The Galiuros are straight across the valley to the northeast. Their high point, Bassett Peak, appears as a bump on the southern end of the range. Across the San Pedro River rise the granite formations of the Cochise Stronghold in the Dragoon Mountains. Dos Cabezas are visible as a single nipple in the distance past the Dragoons. The bumpy ridgecrest of the Chiricahuas rises in the east. The Mule Mountains sit just across the valley at the base of Miller Peak. The most striking summit nearby is Mexico's Sierra San Jose, just over the border in the southeast.

Access: About 14 miles south of Sierra Vista, Highway 92 bends east. Just after this bend, at milepost 334.9, turn south onto Coronado Memorial Road. Coronado Memorial Road turns into Montezuma Canyon Road, and turns to dirt about 6 miles from the highway. The road climbs Montezuma Canyon, arriving at Montezuma Pass about 8.5 miles from Highway 92. There is a large parking area and rest rooms at Montezuma Pass. The Miller Peak Trail starts at the pass, on the north side of the road.

La ruta de immagracion

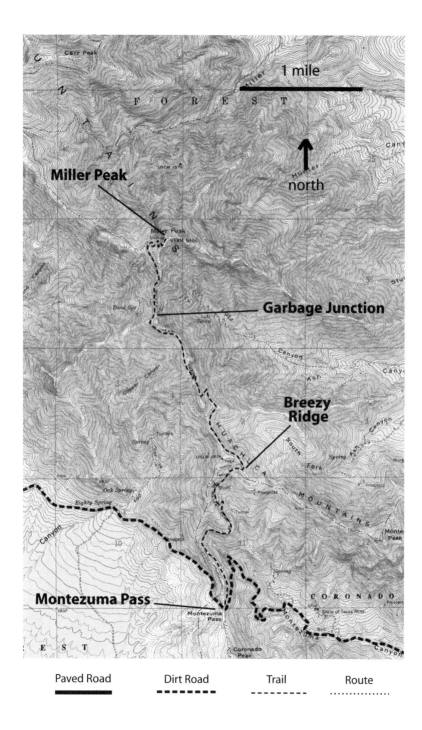

1 mile

north

Miller Peak

Garbage Junction

Breezy
Ridge

Montezuma Pass

Paved Road   Dirt Road   Trail   Route

Wasson Peak

HIKE

General Description: A trail hike to the high point of the Tucson Mountains
Summit Elevation: 4,687'
Vertical Gain: 1,787'
Round-Trip Distance: 8 miles
Optimal Season: November — March
Route Surface and Difficulty: Maintained trail

Perched at the edge of the city, this is *Arizona Summits'* obligatory Tucson mountain. That's not to say that a hike up Wasson Peak isn't fantastic. The trails are gentle, the scenery is pleasant, and the view from the top is more expansive than you might think for a small mountain just a few miles from downtown.

Geologically, the range is so messed up that there is a rock unit here officially called the Tucson Mountain Chaos. At the top of Wasson Peak, the substrate is granite. Lower on the mountain, the rocks are volcanic tuff, sedimentary floodplain deposits, schist, sandstone, and limestone—chaos.

The botanical community is a menagerie as well. Nearly all the Sonoran Desert's trademark plants are here: olive green jojoba, stunning yellow flowered brittlebush, spreading prickly pear cactus and tall saguaros, elegant slender-armed ocotillos, dark green creosote bushes, and green stick-like palo verdes—the state tree.

There are a few different routes through Tucson Mountain Park to the top of Wasson Peak. The one described here, the King Valley Trail, is the shortest way to the summit. It begins at the back of a dirt parking lot located across the road from the Sonoran Desert Museum.

Don't start down the trail that heads into the creekbed adjacent to the parking lot. Rather, head up an old road from the back of the lot that leads to a trail map kiosk in less than 100 yards. After a quick perusal of the park map, continue up the old roadbed as it makes a gradual climb, and then descends into a wash about 1 mile from the kiosk.

After following the wash for about 100 yards, the trail turns up a short stone stairway. This leads into a long gradual climb as the footpath ascends desert slopes. At about 2.5 miles, a saddle and trail junction are reached, with a view of Tucson to the east. The peak looming above the saddle is not Wasson. Bummer! This is an unnamed ridge high point, and the trail traverses just below it en route to Wasson Peak. The climb from the saddle to the high ridge is the steepest part of the route, followed by a 0.3 mile traverse over to the domed summit of Wasson Peak.

Wasson Peak Trail on the verge of Tucson

Picacho Peak sits across the Santa Cruz Flats to the north. The spire-thumb of Baboquivari sticks up in the southwest, and the Kitt Peak telescopes are visible at the north end of that same range. The Sierrita Mountains are nearly due south. The peaked summit of Mt. Wrightson sits on the far side of Tucson to the south-southwest, while towering Rincon Peak and hulking Mica Mountain rise over the city in the east.

Access: Take Highway 86—Ajo Way—west from Tucson, following signs for Old Tucson and Saguaro National Park. At milepost 166.3, turn north on Kinney Road, and follow it 7.6 miles to a dirt parking lot on the northeast side of the road at the King Valley Trailhead. This lot is located just past the entrance to the Sonoran Desert Museum, across the road.

Ferocactus, Lisa, Wasson

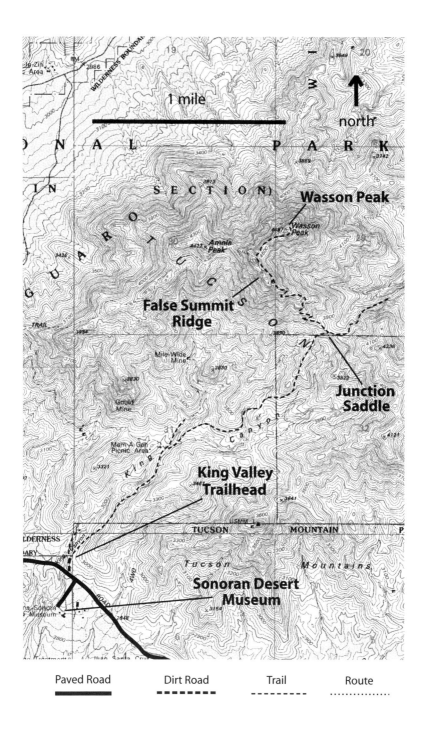

1 mile

north

Wasson Peak

False Summit Ridge

Junction Saddle

King Valley Trailhead

Sonoran Desert Museum

Paved Road ——— Dirt Road -------- Trail --------- Route ....

Mt. Ajo

HIKE

General Description: A trail hike in a unique portion of the Sonoran Desert, leading to the high point of the Ajo Mountains
Summit Elevation: 4,808'
Vertical Gain: 2,450'
Round-Trip Distance: 9 miles
Optimal Season: November — March
Route Surface and Difficulty: Trail with two short steep sections

Arizona's Mountains, a book that served as an inspiration for this one, displays a photo of a pinnacled desert peak on the cover. The cover peak is labeled within the book's copyright page, somewhat surreptitiously, as "Ajo Mountain." Assuming the pointy peak was Mt. Ajo, I quickly put it on the hot list for inclusion here. But assuming only makes an ass out of..well you know. It wasn't until I stood on the breezy summit of Mt. Ajo that I realized the old cover photo was certainly of the Ajo Mountains, but it was most certainly not the range's high point, Mt. Ajo. Tillotson Peak farther north is the most likely suspect, a peak whose zenith I have yet to reach. Still, the somewhat less striking Mt. Ajo provides a great hike to the highest point around.

The route to Mt. Ajo begins on the maintained Bull Pasture Trail. This trail climbs 850 feet in 1.5 miles, reaching a ridge viewpoint that overlooks Bull Pasture—a basin scored with drainages sitting beneath colorful sculpted cliffs of the Ajo Range. From the Bull Pasture viewpoint, Mt. Ajo appears as the highest peak to the left, with striated yellow cliffs just beneath the summit.

Beyond the overlook, the trail is less groomed, but still easy to follow with plentiful cairns. Initially, it descends slightly before leading to the back of the Bull Pasture basin. The route then curves east and northeast, making a mellow traversing ascent across the basin toward the main brushy gulch east of Bull Pasture. Here the trail climbs more steeply, leading between uniquely eroded outcops, and passing a rock window near the top of the crux 400' climb. At the 4,000' elevation, an ascending traverse begins again as the trail stays just below the ridge crest, finally breaking over the top at 4,350'.

Once the ridge is gained, the route traverses to the east slopes of the range as it bypasses a dark gray false summit knob. Low cliffbands split the trail into a few different routes through here, but all paths soon reunite to follow the Ajo Range divide. The trail eventually climbs the gentle east face of Mt. Ajo.

In the southwest, the Gulf of California, or Sea of Cortez, can be seen on

Camping beneath the Ajo Range

some days. At other times, the sea hides beneath an obscuring fog. The Mexican town of Sonoyta sits in the foreground valley, with Sierra Chubabi rising behind town. In the east, the sentinel of Baboquivari rises over the low deserts. At the north end of that range, good eyes will be able to depict telescopes atop Kitt Peak. In a gap north of the Baboquivari Range, distant Rincon Peak rises to a pointy summit. The Santa Catalinas, and their high point bump of Mt. Lemmon forms the horizon farther north. The jagged Silver Bell Mountains are to the left, with eminent Gu Achi towering over desert lands closer to Mt. Ajo. On clear days, the Pinal Mountains are visible far to the northeast. Table Top Mountain, the highest landform in the north, and Woolsey Peak, a dome shaped mountain also to the north, are usually both recognizable. In the west, gently sloped Kino Mountain dominates the landscape.

Overhead, fighter jets sometimes practice dogfights.

Access: Take Highway 85 south from Ajo, Arizona about 30 miles to Organ Pipe National Park. In 2009, it was $8 to enter the park. The trail to Mt. Ajo is located off Ajo Mountain Drive, which starts across the highway from the park visitor center. It is a decent dirt road for most of its 21 mile loop, with some sections paved. Eleven miles down the one-way road is the Bull Pasture / Estes Canyon Trailhead.

Camping at the trailhead is not permitted. The nearest camping is in the park campground—$12 a night. There is often a checkpoint with armed soldiers and dogs on Highway 85 north of Ajo.

Rock window along the Mt. Ajo route

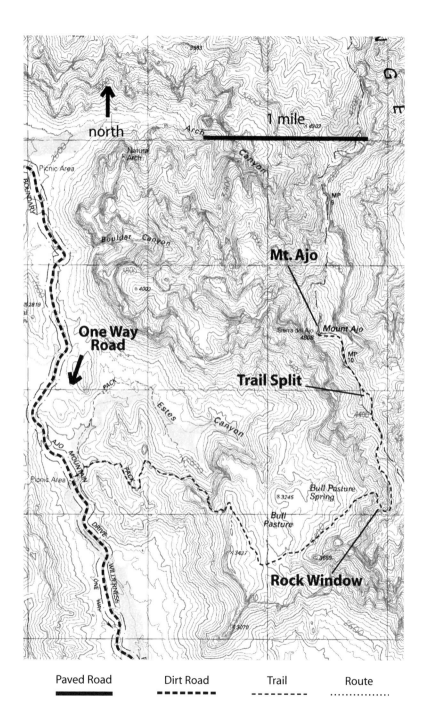

Paved Road   Dirt Road   Trail   Route

SCRAMBLES

Camelback Mountain

HIKE / SCRAMBLE

General Description: A busy summit route in an urban setting
Summit Elevation: 2,704'
Vertical Gain: 1,300'
Round-Trip Distance: 3 miles
Optimal Season: November — March, early mornings during hotter weather
Route Surface and Difficulty: Stairway trail / 3rd class bedrock with hand-rail / Well-used 3rd class route over rough rocks

This is urban Arizona summiting at its best. Throngs of energetic hikers make the climb up Camelback Mountain daily, braving a rugged route to gain a beautiful and notable summit. Camelback is home to headphone-clad aerobic junkies who run up the mountain, steadfast geriatrics who take it one step at a time, toddlers who brave the relatively monumental distance, strolling home boyz, and happy Labrador retrievers. Cell phones are common here too, often used to relay trail conditions to expedition members pinned down on the lower slopes of the mountain. Avalanches and altitude sickness aren't as hazardous at Camelback as in the Himalaya, but the traffic jams and surveillance cameras are infinitesimally worse.

The trail begins as a series of broad stairs leading up a rocky amphitheater. The northwest "camel's hump" of the mountain often shades this part of the climb, and the setting is intimate and canyon like. A notch with a view eastward signals the end of this first section, and serves as a good turn-around spot for those not committed to make the summit.

After the notch, the trail traverses along a vertical cliff, with a tall fence providing protection for dizzied hikers, and preventing excessive erosion caused by straying feet. The crux of the route comes at the far end of this traverse, where a long handrail offers assistance up a pitch of polished bedrock. Above the handrail-aided crux, welcome views are gained as the trail straddles a ridge. Another steep section follows the ridge respite, where a broad gully of boulders requires good balance to ascend. Fortunately, the gully is wide enough to accommodate a variety of summiters of all speeds. The slope eases, but the boulders continue for the last part of trail to the summit.

The view from the top can be quite good, especially if you're able to catch it on a day of low air pollution. The Four Peaks, Sierra Estrellas, White Tanks, and Bradshaw Mountains are almost always visible. On good days, one can spot the distant Santa Catalinas near Tucson.

The Valley's in-town mountain

Access: From Freeway 101 in Scottsdale, take McDonald Drive west for about 5 miles to Echo Canyon Parkway. Turn south on Echo Canyon Parkway and proceed a couple hundred yards to a parking area.

From Phoenix, take 44th Street north past Camelback Road until it turns east and becomes McDonald. Proceed 0.3 miles to a stoplight, and stay right on McDonald, then right again onto Echo Canyon Parkway. The parking area is a couple hundred yards up the hill.

On busy days, the Echo Canyon lot fills up quickly, and most streets in the area are rife with no parking signs. Hikers burdened with an automobile sometimes must venture a mile or more from the trailhead to find a parking spot.

There is a small public parking area about 0.4 miles west of Echo Canyon on McDonald. This cul-de-sac is located just inside the Phoenix city limits, on McDonald Drive where it turns north at 44th Street.

Sotol and Weavers Needle

Off route under the spell of Baboquivari

Descending from the land of fhe Gods

The multi-day Cathedral Rock route

Aspens in the Galiuros

Abbey's view

Tucson from Wasson Peak
(Cathedral Rock and Mt. Lemmon in background)

A December morning on Signal Peak

Looking through Mt. Ajo

Rainbow Valley west of the Sierra Estrellas—a lot like Nevada, with saguaros

Overlooking the San Rafael Valley grasslands from Miller Peak

November colors en route to Bassett Peak

Southern Arizona mountaineering lacks glacial crevasses,
but it has other hazards.

Atop the top Eagle Tail

Checkin' the exposure on Weavers Needle

Nowhere but Arizona

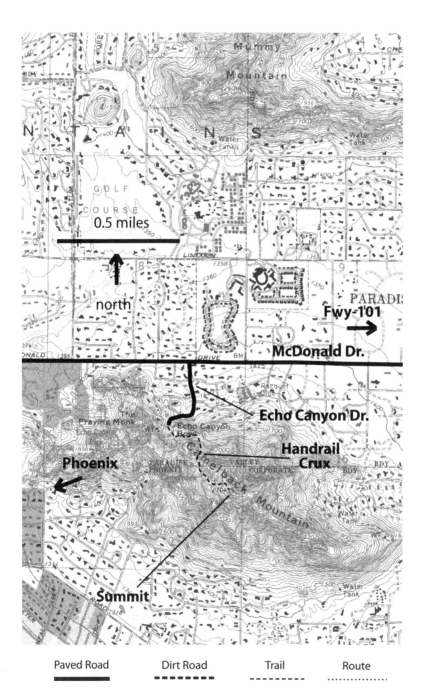

Paved Road   Dirt Road   Trail   Route

Big Horn Peak

SCRAMBLE

General Description: A rocky hike to the prominent high point of the Big Horn Mountains
Summit Elevation: 3,480'
Vertical Gain: 2,080'
Round-Trip Distance: 7 miles
Optimal Season: November — March
Route Surface and Difficulty: Off trail flat desert / semi-loose 2nd class hiking / 3rd class semi-loose side-hillling with cholla / 30' 4th class scramble

Big Horn Peak cuts a classic silhouette against the desert skyline, luring an array of aspiring mountaineers to its slopes. In the summit register, a memorable entry is recorded, documenting perhaps the most ambitious Big Horn ascent ever, and illustrating the spirit of adventure.

After gazing at the pinnacle of Big Horn for over three years from his position at the Palo Verde Nuclear Generating Station, an employee could deny his curiosity no more. He set out at 3 a.m. on a straight-line trudge to the base of the mountain. By daybreak he was making a dash across Interstate 10, where he narrowly missed becoming yet another discarded road kill along the route to Los Angeles. Undaunted, the intrepid explorer continued, only to find his route blocked by a great canal.

The aqueduct ran as far as the eye could see in either direction. Its banks were steep and smooth, and the water it carried was cold, deep, and swift. The obstacle was great, but the call of the mountain was strong, and the trailblazer jumped in with barely a hesitation. The man floated lazily with the stream, enjoying a respite from gravity as the desert hills receded beyond his new world of blue water and white concrete. He stroked to the far side to crawl out of the water ditch, but he found that a slimy algae prevented him from stopping himself along the side of the canal. The current pushed him persistently along. There was no purchase for his feet in the deep water, and he clawed impotently at the smooth wet concrete at water's edge. He began to fatigue.

The man looked ahead to see what his fate might reveal. Downstream, to the east, the canal ran straight into a mountain, disappearing. His motivation to leave the water was now stronger than ever. He pushed himself away from the concrete bank to regain his wits, and gain a better view. Ahead was a seam in the concrete where his fingers might gain a hold. He drifted towards the uniform crack, breast stroked to the edge, and at the last instant lunged for the indentation. The first digits of his fingers found a hold, and

On route on Big Horn

he stopped himself against the pull of current. Working his hands slowly up the seam, he got a knee out of the water and onto dry concrete above the water line. Next he got a foot up, and seconds later he was standing atop the concrete levee, wet, alone, and alive.

Following his canal epic, Mr. Palo Verde strolled up Big Horn Peak with relative ease, arriving at the summit with nightfall. His story is told with brevity in the summit register.

The canal that nearly drowned our intrepid explorer is restricted, but bridges across the waterway provide foot-travel corridors at a few places. One of these bridges serves as the initial approach to Big Horn Peak. Be sure to close the barbed wire gate behind you when you cross.

Once beyond the north canal levee, follow a fence line north for about 200 yards until it turns east, and make your way east / northeast toward the mountain. There are some barricaded historical ruins you might notice en route. Other than these industrial remnants, there are few distractions on the flat 2 mile trudge to the base of the mountain.

The route follows the south ridge up rocky, moderately steep desert slopes until reaching a promontory at 2,200'. Here, the terrain flattens for the next half-mile, providing pleasant walking with nice views to the east. When the south ridge is swallowed by the mountainside at 2,600', the climb gets steeper. Occasional 4th class scrambling might be required to avoid terrifying cholla thickets and/or loose traverses. The most moderate route leads west before angling back northeast. A vague gully, sometimes with cairns, leads up the mountain to a notch just east of the summit. The final 50 feet from here to the top is the most difficult part of the route. A northeast facing crack (difficult 4th class) will deliver climbers to the breezy summit.

The Eagletail Mountains are most apparent directly across the Harquahala Plain to the south, with the pinnacled Kofa Mountains farther to the southwest. Harquahala Mountain sits nearby to the northwest. With binoculars, Hyde Peak is sometimes visible as a rounded twin summit far to the north. The Bradshaw Mountains cover the skyline to the northeast. Just slightly south of due east are the White Tank Mountains. If the air quality is good, the Superstitions are discernible due east, beyond the Phoenix smudge. Saddle Mountain cuts a jagged V on the southeastern horizon in the middle distance, with the flat-topped dome of Woolsey Peak rising in the distance beyond.

Access: Take I-10 west from Phoenix to exit #81—Salome Road. Turn right on Salome Road and continue 0.5 miles before again turning right onto a wide dirt road. Follow this road, bending west, then north along a canal and fence until running into the Central Arizona Canal about 3.5 miles from Salome Road. Bear right (east) at the canal, and park in about 100 yards, near a foot bridge that crosses the canal.

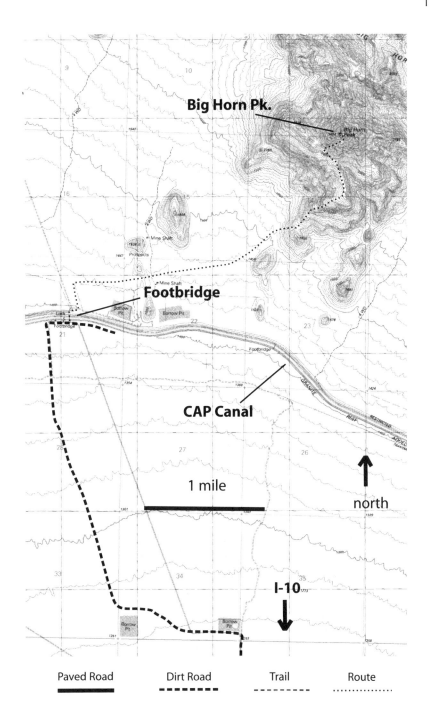

Big Horn Pk.

Footbridge

CAP Canal

1 mile

north

I-10

Paved Road   Dirt Road   Trail   Route

Picacho Peak

HIKE / SCRAMBLE

General Description: An aided route up a noted Arizona landmark
Summit Elevation: 3,374'
Vertical Gain: 1,374'
Round-Trip Distance: 4 miles
Optimal Season: November — March
Route Surface and Difficulty: Rocky steep maintained trail / near vertical 4th class trail festooned with cables

Picacho Peak has been a sentinel in the Arizona desert for centuries. Native inhabitants likely used the recognizable butte as a navigation tool, Jesuit priest Father Kino wrote about the peak in his journals, stage routes forged past the foot of the mountain, railroad tracks followed suit, and today Interstate 10 runs along the base of Picacho Peak. Modern day travelers who are intrigued by the characteristic shape of this landmark will be pleased to learn that a climb to the summit is as spectacular as it looks.

This is Arizona's very own via ferrata route, with cables and iron bars anchored into the mountain along the steeper sections of the climb. Via ferrata is Italian for "iron road," and the constructed climbing routes are common in Italy's Dolomite Mountains. Although the presence of permanent metal hardware might be incongruous with many wilderness hiking trails in the United States, the rustic handrails seem to fit the scene here at Picacho, where the din of the freeway is never far away.

The trail begins by climbing toward volcanic cliffs guarding the east side of the peak. Cable handrails assist in the ascent where some rocky slabs steepen the terrain. The rocky but well maintained trail leads to a saddle at 2,960' before making a disheartening descent onto the quiet (opposite the freeway) side of the mountain. This is where the cables strung between rebar come in handy, as the route follows loose and steep terrain along the base of a crumbling cliff.

A mellower traverse follows, and the Sunset Vista Trail comes in from below to intersect the summit-bound Hunter Trail. Not far beyond the fork, the route climbs more steeply as it approaches a near vertical section of rock adorned with hardware—the crux of the route. Were the cables not present, this would be 5th class climbing. As it exists, the climb is accessible to a wide range of determined and careful hikers. Gloves can sometimes help with ascending the unyielding cables.

At the top of the crux, the trail leads to the back of a tilted basin before reaching another cable-aided climb that is nearly as hard as the crux. By

Ruth the inspiring one on Picacho

now the scent of the summit is in the air (or is that the manure from the farms below?), and few will be deterred by the final aided traverse across a north facing cliff. Emerging onto the summit slope, the sounds of commerce quickly return for the final walk to the top.

The summit view is wonderful. Pinal Mountain stands alone in the northeast, and the Santa Catalinas dominate the southern skyline. To the right of the Catalinas, Mt. Wrightson and its companion Mt. Hopkins are visible, with the spike of Baboquivari peeking out from an array of rugged mountains to the southwest.

Access: Take exit #219 off Interstate 10 and follow signs to Picacho Peak State Park. In 2009, there was a $6 entrance fee per vehicle. The nearest trailhead for the summit, the Hunter Trail, is located at the end of Barrett Loop road.

The assisted crux on Picacho Peak's fixed route

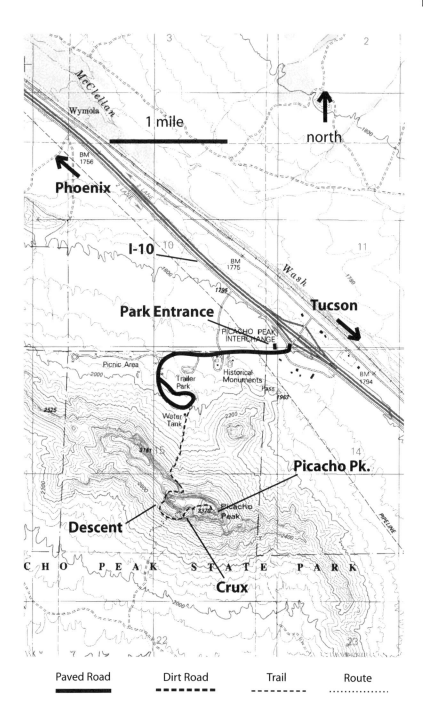

Castle Dome Peak

HIKE / SCRAMBLE

General Description: A varied route up a dramatic desert peak
Summit Elevation: 3,788'
Vertical Gain: 2,088'
Round-Trip Distance: 7 miles
Optimal Season: November — March
Route Surface and Difficulty: Sand and gravel streambed / loose scree and talus / 3rd and 4th class scrambling on moderately stable rock

Castle Dome Peak pokes above the horizon like an eminent crown over the rest of its namesake range. It is the type of natural landform that attracts the attention of passersby, and beckons the curious. When mountaineers approach the mountain, gaining a closer view of the peak from the north, they are stopped by an even more striking shape. Castle Dome Peak has beautiful lines, and a climb to its summit has everything one might expect from such a sculpted desert mountain.

The first part of the route is a less than romantic slog up a gravel wash. In the first half-mile, make sure you don't get drawn into minor washes leading south. The main wash leading to Castle Dome Peak stays north of a volcanic peninsula shaped like a double camel hump, located about 0.5 miles from the road.

The approach to the peak continues up the wash until about 2 miles from the road, when cairns will direct you to the south side of the dry creek bottom. A trail starts up the northwest slopes of the mountain here, just before the wash enters an arroyo of vertical cutbanks lining the north side. If the wash begins to narrow, steepen, and become boulder-choked, you've gone too far.

Once out of the wash, a scan of Castle Dome Peak's imposing north face will reveal the thoroughly cairned route. It leads up gradual northwest facing slopes before threading a gap through a band of rock buttresses halfway up the mountain. Above here, the route climbs loose talus en route to the base of the peak's dark north facing cliffs. Traversing the base of these cliffs, it then leads to a notch between the mountain and a noticeable gendarme.

At the notch between the gendarme and the main mountain, there is a fifth class (30' - 5.2) climb leading up to the right, but an easier route also exists. Just 15 feet back down the route, below the notch to the northwest, there is a short 4th class scramble leading up 20 feet of good finger and toe holds.

Above this crux, the route traverses left past a rock window and an over-

Ascending past the gendarme on Castle Dome Peak

hang before again leading upward. There are a few different route options for the last few hundred feet to the summit ridge, all of which are 3rd class. Veering north generally leads to cleaner but steeper lines.

From the top, you can see Yuma, along with Mittry and Martinez Lakes on the Colorado River. On a clear winter day, you might spot the snow covered San Jacintos near Palm Springs to the northwest. The nearby Kofas block distant views to the north, but hulking Harquahala Mountain is visible to the northeast, and rounded Woolsey Peak rises from the haze in the east. Close by, tethered in space, is an eerie white blimp.

Access: Turn off Highway 95 onto Castle Dome Road at milepost 55. In 2 miles, this paved road turns abruptly to dirt. Continue straight. About 9 miles from the highway, there is a fork. Again, continue straight toward Mcpherson Pass. In less than a mile, you will pass the Castle Dome Mines Museum, and the road degrades slightly. At 1.6 miles past the museum, bear left at a fork. In another 2 miles, the road makes a sharp left at a broad wash after making a steady gradual climb. This wash is the parking area for the route. GPS coordinates: N33°05.914' W114°10.513'

Castle Dome Peak

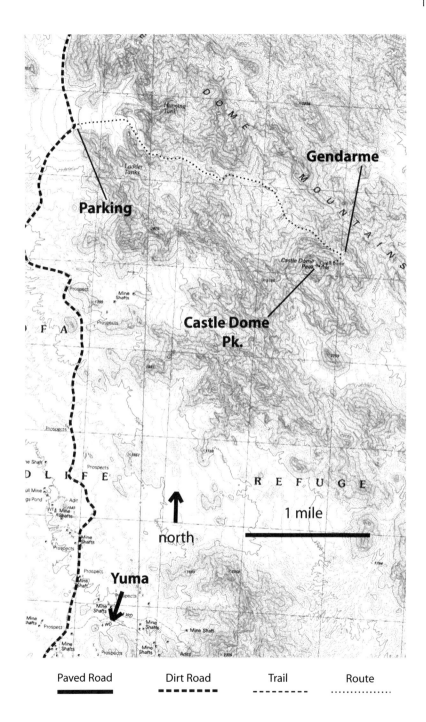

| Paved Road | Dirt Road | Trail | Route |

Woolsey Peak

SCRAMBLE

General Description: An off-trail route through boulders to a broad summit
Summit Elevation: 3,171'
Vertical Gain: 1,990'
Round-Trip Distance: 5 miles
Optimal Season: November — March
Route Surface and Difficulty: Cobble road / 3rd class over small marginally-stable boulders / thick cholla

Visually, Woolsey Peak is one of the most prominent mountains in Arizona, visible from many different locales throughout the southern deserts. The shape of the mountain is strikingly reminiscent of Mt. Rainier, the most prominent mountain in the lower forty eight states at 14,410', rising from a base elevation of only 1,200 feet. The base of Woolsey is also roughly 1,200', with a summit elevation about 2,000' higher. It's not in the same league as Rainier, but a hike to the top of Woolsey Peak makes for a stellar outing in a relatively wild desert region.

Starting due north of the peak at the 1180' map indication, a road follows a fence line straight towards the hulking form of the mountain. After gently gaining a few hundred feet in elevation, the road gives way to a relentless boulder field that will accompany you for the remainder of the way to the summit.

Not far above the end of the road, it's best to angle southwest toward a saddle between Woolsey and "peak 2030." From the saddle below peak 2,030', it is a straight shot up 900 feet of black rocks, any one of which could easily snap an ankle. With careful foot placement, however, the intimidating talus can be a stairway of basalt leading up the mountain. The boulder slope reaches a pinch point between steep bluffs at 2,600'.

The last 500 feet from the pinch to the summit rim requires a zig-zag course through blocky small cliffs. Spiny vegetation becomes more of a factor, and finding your preferred route takes careful consideration.

Most will reach the summit rim at a point somewhere northeast of the true summit. Walking is flat and relatively easy once on top, but a treacherous plain of Teddy Bear Cholla (Opuntia bigelovii) will dictate your wanderings. There is a benchmark indicating "Gila Peak" on the high point. I was unable to find a summit register.

Due west on the horizon, Castle Dome Peak is a thumb-like butte. North of this, Signal Peak of the Kofa Mountains appears more like a dome. Northwest and nearby are the tan crags of Signal Mountain. Directly behind

Climbing the Woolsey boulder field

it are the Eagle Tail Mountains. The Palo Verde Nuclear Generating Station releases wastewater steam into the atmosphere in the foreground to the north. The Bradshaw and White Tank Mountains are offset to the northeast. A discerning eye might differentiate the Verde Rim from the Mazatzal Range farther east. The southern Mazatzal's Mt. Ord and Four Peaks are more easily spotted. The Sierra Estrella skyline usually rises above a smoggy lowland just south of east. The Gila Bend Mountains, of which Woolsey Peak is the high point, serve as the peak's foothills to the southeast.

Access: Take Highway 85 south from I-10 about 6 miles and turn west onto Old U.S. 80 before crossing the Gila River. Take Old 80 about 15 miles southwest, past the towns of Hassayampa and Arlington, and head west on Agua Caliente Road at milepost 25.2. If you are coming from the south on Old 80, Agua Caliente Road is about 3 miles north of the bridge over the Gila River near Gillespie Dam.

Take paved Agua Caliente Road 0.6 miles, and turn right onto a major dirt road. In 0.15 miles, turn left onto a smaller dirt road heading toward Woolsey Peak.

Officially unnamed, we'll call this Woolsey Peak Road, as it leads directly to the peak. There are several forks diverging from this road. Don't be lured. Remain on the main road heading south toward the mountain, and in about 7 miles you'll be at the start of the hiking route. About 4.8 miles from Agua Caliente Road, Woolsey Peak Road bends around the southwest end of a low mountain range, then runs along a wash before reaching a major fork 6.4 miles from pavement. Continue straight at the fork. There is a short steep climb 0.2 miles farther where most non four-wheel-drives will want to park. If you desire to drive as far as possible, it is another 0.4 miles to a fence line at point 1180', then another 0.7 miles along the fence to the end of the road.

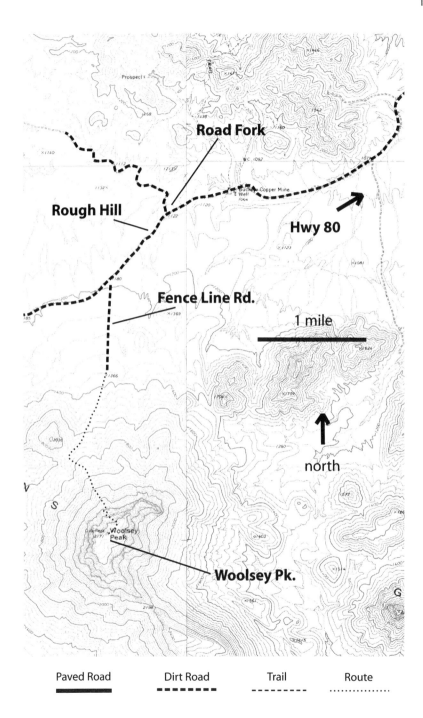

Road Fork

Rough Hill

Fence Line Rd.

Hwy 80

1 mile

north

Woolsey Pk.

| Paved Road | Dirt Road | Trail | Route |

Montezuma Peak

HIKE / SCRAMBLE

General Description: A rugged loop route in the Sierra Estrella Range
Summit Elevation: 4,337'
Vertical Gain: 2,804'
Round-Trip Distance: 7 miles
Optimal Season: November — March
Route Surface and Difficulty: Flat firm sand / large stable boulders / 3rd class steep crumbly granite / 4th class ridge scrambling / moderate cactus and brush

The Sierra Estrellas are an anomaly. They are steep, rugged, and wild. They are also at the doorstep of a city of five million people. On the west side of the range opposite Phoenix, you'd hardly know the city is so close. This is Rainbow Valley, a lonely basin reminiscent of Nevada, but with saguaros.

It is an easy 2-mile walk through these saguaros on valley sediments to the base of the mountains. A mellow ascent begins at the bottom of an alluvial fan adjacent to the peak's west ridge. The fan narrows into a drainage as the mountain's ribs close in, and the hiking upgrades to class 2 and 3, primarily boulder hopping.

To gain the west ridge, leave the drainage at about 2,250 ' and plod north on steeper slopes of semi-loose crumbling granite. Inconveniently placed cacti, mostly Teddy bear and staghorn cholla, complicate the ascent.

Once gaining the west ridge, travel conditions improve, and the view opens dramatically. Steep desert slopes peel away below, and summit buttresses loom above. The ridge route is mostly grade 3, but class 4 scrambling will come in handy at several places where cactus or spiny palo verde trees make the flatter terrain nearby less appealing. Knife edge granite plates often offer the best route.

The narrow ridge continues until reaching a small, flat, picnic-spot saddle just below a steep granite buttress guarding the summit. I tried to climb directly up the buttress, and wouldn't recommend it. After hacking up a narrow alleyway to an armless saguaro, the route becomes a series of vegetation choked ledges among cliffs, not real appealing.

Instead, traverse right from the picnic saddle, and climb up the partially bedrock infused gully to the east / southeast. You will invariably wind up in the proverbial steep, loose gully, but it's neither too steep nor too loose. Soon you will emerge on the range crest, with a shocking cityscape in the near distance.

One ridge up, one ridge down—descending from the summit of Montezuma Pk.

A nice 4th class scramble leads to the summit from here. To the north is a peak with solar arrays on top. To the south is a flat area with a communication tower. In a tin is a summit register, where you might indulge your alter ego nickname in the themed notebook.

A good descent option follows the southwest ridge. Beyond the nearby radio tower, the ridge is considerably less steep than the west ridge of the ascent. There is some side-hilling necessary to circumvent ridge knobs, but travel is certainly faster than the steep and narrow west ridge. From a quartz rock saddle before the last ridge hump, you can descend to the north or south, and then slog across the flats back to your basecamp.

Access: Take Highway 347 (Maricopa Road) to Highway 238. Head west on 238 for about 9 miles, and turn right on San Rafael (sometimes called simply Rafael) Road. This turn is at approximately milepost 35.6. Follow San Rafael Road north and northeast for 2.7 miles, and turn left onto a secondary dirt road heading north. In about 1 mile, bear right at a fork. (I think the left fork works here too.) At 1.8 miles from San Rafael Road, stay left at another fork. Park about 5 miles from San Rafael Road, in the vicinity of: N33°.08.689′ W111°.13.567′.

By continuing another couple miles, one can find four-wheel-drive roads that get closer to the base of the west ridge. There is also a sandy dirt track that gets closer to the foot of the southwest ridge, but it is often washed out, and only saves 0.75 miles of flat easy walking.

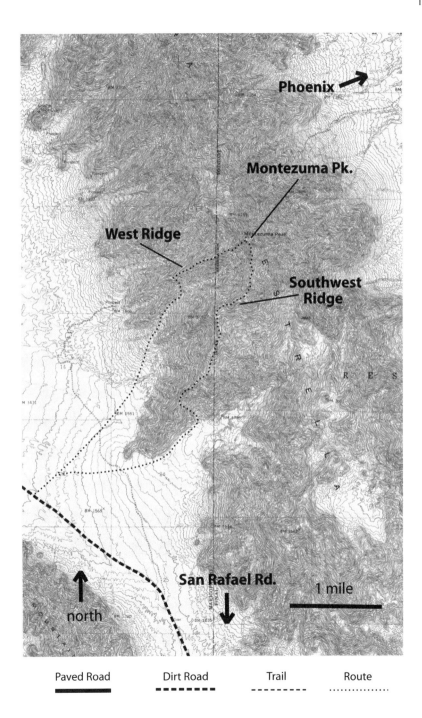

Phoenix

Montezuma Pk.

West Ridge

Southwest Ridge

San Rafael Rd.

1 mile

north

Paved Road	Dirt Road	Trail	Route

Window Peak

SCRAMBLE

General Description: A short, steep, unique route in the aptly named Sawtooth Mountains
Summit Elevation: 2,630'
Vertical Gain: 930'
Round-Trip Distance: 2 miles
Optimal Season: November — March
Route Surface and Difficulty: Off trail desert / 4th class scrambling with moderate brush / easy 5th class climbing with exposure

This is one of those pleasant little gems hiding in the Arizona rough. Viewed from busy Interstate 10, the Sawtooth Mountains cut a jagged knife edge skyline. It was this horizon that intrigued me to first seek out the mountains, and when I consulted Bob and Dotty Martin's book *Arizona's Mountains*, my interest was further piqued. Their brief description reads; "Hike northwest to gain an airy ridge...passing over a natural arch on the way to the summit." Talk about veiled titillation.

To the east of the peak, gentle slopes surround the lower mountain. The going gets steeper with some minor side-hilling required on the way to the first major goal of the route—a narrow gunsight saddle south of the main peak. From here things get steeper yet, as the route leads directly up 4th class ledges to the north, following the mountain's ridgeline. A steep razor back ridge forms above here, while the route stays on easier terrain just west of the jagged rock fin. When a broad saddle connecting a knob-hill appears to the left (northwest), traverse over to it. Continuing up the ridge, although tempting, only leads to an isolated crag.

From the broad knob-connecting saddle, contour another hundred yards or so until a cliffband forces you to ascend a southwest facing 3rd class gully. At the top of the gully, there is an arch, often with a steady breeze funneling through. The route, unbelievably, goes up 4th class rock to the right (south), and crosses a narrow neck of rock directly above the arch.

The crux move of the route comes next, as you move up the ridge on the north side of the arch. The exposure is significant, and at least one 5th class maneuver is required to proceed. Just a few moves more will pop you out onto the broad upper shoulder of the mountain, where the walking is leisurely. There is one more scramble just below the summit, but the exposure is limited.

The first signature in the summit register is that of Dick Langley, and it is through his suggestion that I've called the mountain "Window Peak." He

Window Peak Route

proclaimed, "I've been up here umpteen times...I call it Window Peak." Fair enough Dick, Window Peak sounds better than "Peak 2,630."

If you're concerned about down climbing the arch route, there is a mellower 3rd and 4th class way to descend on the western slopes of the mountain.

Access: Anywhere near the eastern base of the mountains can serve as a starting point for this route. There is a north to south trending road that serves as the primary access, with a few spur roads branching off, and leading closer to the range.

To reach the primary access road, there are approaches from the north, south, and east. Each is a convoluted course around private property, and over rough terrain. Below is the description of the east approach, which is the simplest route, I swear.

Take Sunland Gin Road south from I-10 at exit 200, and go almost 16 miles to Pearce Road. Take Pearce Road west for 1.6 miles and turn north on a road running between farm fields. Follow this 1 mile to a levee, and a hard left. From the hard left, proceed southwest 0.7 miles, and turn right (west / northwest) on a road that cuts over the levee through some stout rusty gate anchors. In 0.6 miles past the levee, proceed through a gate and barbed wire fence. In another 0.5 miles, you will intersect the primary access road. Either direction can lead to good access points for the peak. To the right, there is a spur road offering good access in 0.8 miles at: N32°.36.635′ W111°.42.220′. To the left, there is a spur road in 0.2 miles. It is 0.9 miles down this spur road to a wildlife water guzzler at: N32°.36.736′ W111°.43.174′. I parked near here, a respectful distance from the water source, of course.

The Sawtooth Mountains rise over irrigated farms in south-central Arizona.

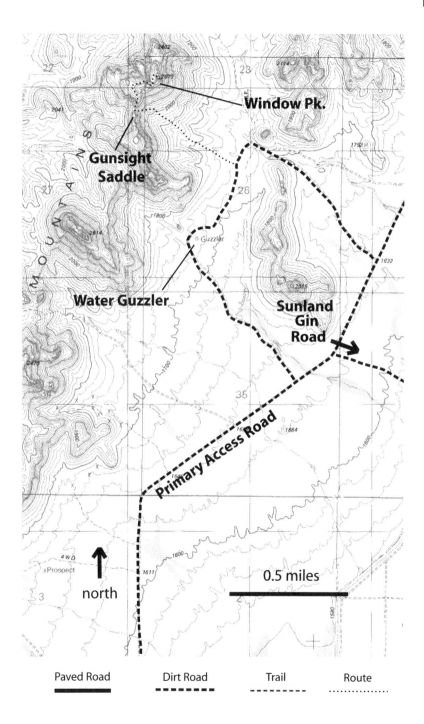

Window Pk.

Gunsight Saddle

Water Guzzler

Guzzler

Sunland Gin Road

Primary Access Road

4WD
xProspect

↑ north

0.5 miles

Paved Road   Dirt Road   Trail   Route

Dos Cabezas

SCRAMBLE

General Description: A short steep climb to two prominent rocky summits
Summit Elevation: North Cabeza—8,354' / South Cabeza—8,357'
Vertical Gain: 2,400'
Round-Trip Distance: 4.5 miles
Optimal Season: March — November / Be wary of thunderstorms over these exposed summits in summertime
Route Surface and Difficulty: Off-trail grassy slopes / heavy brush / 3rd and 4th class scrambling

Dos Cabezas: Two Heads. The twin formations of this Southeastern Arizona landmark can be spotted for many miles. For over a century, the mountain slopes below the rocky summits have been mined for lead, silver, and gold. In the 1880s, a small boom occurred in response to the mines, and a town of over 300 people existed at the base of the mountain range. It's likely that the most adventurous of these early citizens scampered to the top of the Cabezas. Inscriptions on the south summit date back to 1908.

Today, the ghost town is crumbling, but the route to the top of the peaks hasn't changed much. The long rolling southeast ridge serves as the most commonly used approach. From either of the described parking spots, one can quickly gain the southeast ridge and its relatively open grassy slopes. The words open and grassy won't come to mind initially, as the lower portions of the ridge are filled with scratchy southern Arizona desert scrub. Once on the ridge crest, however, the walking improves dramatically.

The ridge reaches a high point at 7,900', where there is a tall radio tower. Once cresting the tower hill, the rocky humps of Dos Cabezas burst suddenly into view. A lovely oak parkland forms a saddle en route to the peaks. Beyond the oak saddle, some rudimentary paths aid in a traverse through the woods to the base of the south Cabeza.

A gorilla trail leads up a gully of low-growing oak near the base of the peak's south face. Near the top of the oak jungle, look for cairns indicating a traverse leading east. Here, you will gratefully bust out of the vegetation onto rock slabs. Follow the gradually ascending traverse around a blind corner until reaching a gully with scattered oaks growing among loose rocks.

This gully leads up to a short 4th class scramble behind a small chokestone. Another 50 yards of simple scrambling to the northwest will have you on the south summit, where a myriad of "cowboy glyphs" serve as a summit register of old timers. In the register for us new timers, you might notice an inordinate amount of references to rattlesnakes encountered along the

Tres Cabezas

route. Watch your step!

To reach the north Cabeza, you can use a 4th class gully that leads to a pass between the peaks. Travel north about 70 feet from the south summit, then curve back east into the gully. Most consider this to be the hardest part of the route. If you're content with reaching the higher south summit, you might save yourself the drama of this descent, and call it a day.

If you're obsessive like me, and you just have to explore the north summit too, you'll find mostly 3rd class ledges leading up the northwest face of this Cabeza.

The quickest descent route is to return to the saddle between the Cabezas, and descend to the east. It's not great, but it is the most logical route. There are nasty locust bushes, deep ground concealing leaf litter, and one short downclimb bordering on 5th class. A few hundred feet down the steep oak covered slope below the saddle, there is an old jeep trail which offers easy passage back to the range divide at 7,200'.

For other descent options, you might consider retracing your steps over the south summit, or descending west from the Cabezas gully and traversing around the north side of the peak until reaching the jeep trail.

Once at the 7,200' range divide, you might use roads to walk back, or drop into the drainage directly below to reach an old mining road that leads to Mascot Mine Road.

Access: From Willcox, AZ, take Route 186 for 14 miles to the town of Dos Cabezas. Turn north on Mascot Mine Road, and stay left at a fork in 0.5 miles. Just beyond the fork, there is a gate indicating private property. Sign in at the register and proceed. In another 1.3 miles, bear right at a fork. In another half-mile (about 2.3 miles from the highway), there is a road that branches left before crossing a drainage and continuing up a hill to the west. This road can serve as a start to the route.

To start here, proceed north and west up this 4WD road to a saddle at 6,250', and climb up the steep slope to the north to gain the southeast ridge.

For a slightly more direct route, continue on Mascot Mine Road for another quarter-mile and park a couple hundred yards short of a locked pipe gate. From here a tough brushy 200 vertical feet will have you on the southeast ridge.

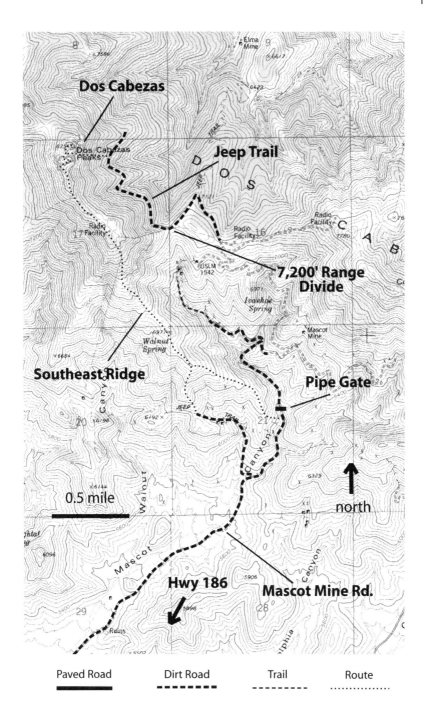

Four Peaks

SCRAMBLE

General Description: A simple hike and scramble to Browns Peak, or a rugged traverse of the entire Four Peaks
Summit Elevation: Browns Peak — 7,657' / Peak #2 — 7,642'
Peak #3 — 7,572' / Peak #4 — 7,524'
Vertical Gain: 1,957' to Browns Peak / 3,115' total vertical to traverse all four peaks
Round-Trip Distance: 6 miles to Browns Pk. / 9 miles for full traverse returning via Amethyst Trail
Optimal Season: late March — April, September — November / Snow in shady gulches makes the route more difficult during winter. Summer brings excessive heat, or dangerous lightning.
Route Surface and Difficulty: Browns — Trail with imbedded boulders / 4th class gully with two low cliffbands requiring short climbs **— Full Traverse** — 4th class downclimbing with heavy brush / 4th to 5th class climbing and exposed ridge traversing

The Four Peaks are perhaps the most recognizable mountain features in Arizona. They cut a dramatic skyline to the east of greater Phoenix, creating an iconic image that adorns the state license plate. A thick blanket of brush covers their slopes, creating habitat for the highest concentration of black bears in the Southwest. Rising above the brushlands are the individual peaks—steep protrusions of Mazatzal Quartzite that loom eminently over the low deserts. Reaching just one or all four summits of the Four Peaks is a classic slice of Arizona mountaineering.

From the trailhead at Lone Pine Saddle, the Four Peaks Trail traverses to the east, while the Browns Peak Trail climbs a ridge en route to the high peaks. Follow this trail of decomposed granite past interesting boulder formations and through a diverse forest to a broad saddle at 5,900'. The trail continues its gentle ascent from here, staying close to a long ridge divide before traversing into dense burned-over brushlands on the east side of the divide. About 2 miles from the trailhead, the trail tops out on a breezy saddle at 6,860', directly below the proud northwest face of Browns Peak.

From the saddle, the trail steepens as it climbs the northwest ridge of the peak, degenerating into a route as it passes gnarled wind blown ponderosa pines. When the ridge thrusts upward into nearly vertical rock, the route merges south into a major gully below an obvious notch on the summit ridge. Incidentally, this notch and gully are visible from the far away dirt roads leading to the trailhead. From afar, look for the first step below the summit to the

The Four Peaks

west, and you will see the dark gash that is the summit-bound gully.

It is about 600 feet up the gully to the notch, leading over mostly 4th class terrain. The route is not exceptionally loose, but there are some inviting hand holds that are ready to pull out with heavy weight. Although I hesitate to call the route 5th class, there are two cliff bands near the top of the gully that are steeper than the rest, and some hikers might want a rope belay, especially for downclimbing on the return. At the top of the gully, bear left and scramble another 100 yards to the summit.

Looking north down the spine of the Mazatzal Range, Mt. Ord and Mazatzal Peak are almost in line from this angle. On clear days, the San Francisco Peaks can be seen on the far horizon just to the right of the aforementioned peaks. Perhaps the most striking summit in view is Mt. Turnbull, rising to a tipped point in the east.

For you maniacs who are up for a full day of scrambling, climbing, and bushwhacking, a traverse of all four peaks will satisfy your cravings. The descent to the saddle between Browns and peak #2 is the worst combination of brush and steep loose rock on the entire route, although there is plenty of each surrounding all four peaks.

The crux of the Four Peaks traverse is getting from the summit of #2 to the summit of #3. We descended to the east, downclimbing sloping slabs that are slide-for-life territory when wet. At the 7,000' contour, there is a cairned route at a slight bench that leads to the #2 / #3 saddle. From here, the broken west face of peak #3 offers many fine routes of 4th and easy 5th class difficulty.

Between peaks #3 and #4, the ridge crest can be followed part way before forcing you to the east slopes, where a brushy traverse will lead to the final saddle. The route up peak #4 is not as steep as the others, but it has more vegetation.

The quickest return route leads down a brushy gully to the west from the peak #3 / #4 saddle, but this leads to the private property of Amethyst Mine. One could return to the #2 / #3 saddle and descend west (again, down a brushy gully) to reach the Amethyst Trail, or descend the northeast ridge of peak #4 to a three-forked basin below Alder Saddle, and pick up the overgrown Alder Trail. This offers a long return via the Alder and Four Peaks Trails.

Access: The west approach follows Road #143 from Highway 87 near milepost 204. It is a rough 18 miles (passable to high clearance vehicles only) to the Mazatzal divide and Road #648. Follow #648 to the south for about 2 miles to the Lone Pine Trailhead.

From the east, access is via the smoother El Oso Road. This leaves Highway 188 at milepost 255.1, near the northwestern arm of Roosevelt Lake. Four miles from the highway, El Oso Road takes a steep turn to the right as it cuts a winding bobsled course into the Mazatzals. About 8.5 miles in, bear left toward Lone Pine Saddle. In another mile, bear left again onto road #648, and follow it about 2 miles to its terminus at Lone Pine Saddle.

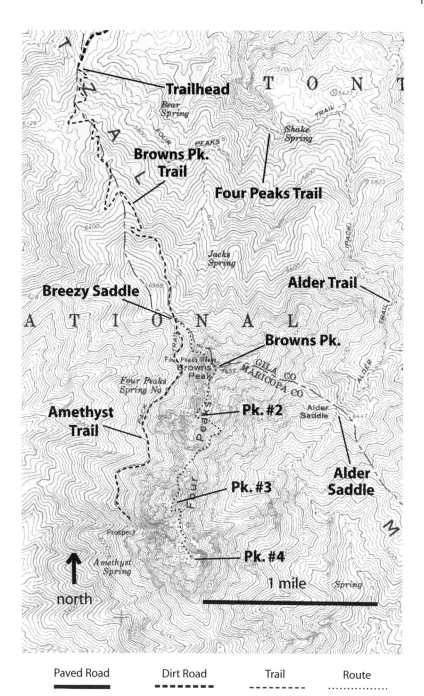

Trailhead

Browns Pk. Trail

Four Peaks Trail

Alder Trail

Breezy Saddle

Browns Pk.

Amethyst Trail

Pk. #2

Alder Saddle

Pk. #3

Pk. #4

1 mile

north

| Paved Road | Dirt Road | Trail | Route |

Cathedral Rock

SCRAMBLE

General Description: A multi-day ascent of the Santa Catalina's most striking summit
Summit Elevation: 7,957'
Vertical Gain: 5,100' from Sabino Canyon visitor center / 4,600' from end of tram road in Sabino Canyon
Round-Trip Distance: 20 miles
Optimal Season: March — April, October — November
Route Surface and Difficulty: Maintained trail / unmaintained trail with cairns / unmaintained trail with deadfall and light brush / route through moderate brush / 4th class climb or single pitch 5th class climb
Fees: $5 per day parking at Sabino Canyon visitor center / $8 shuttle fee for a ride to the end of the road

When looking at the Santa Catalinas from Tucson, the broad blue dome of the range crest doesn't present any obvious mountaineering objectives. Looking to the southwestern flanks of the range, however, a summiter's eye is immediately drawn to a pointed peak standing nobly above the surrounding terrain. This is Cathedral Rock, and reaching its summit is an effort worthy of the mountain's classic form.

There are a few approach options for reaching Cathedral Rock. The Romero Canyon Trail from the west is the longest route, and the Esperero Canyon Trail from the south is the most direct approach. The route described here, the Sabino Basin approach, uses a shuttle service to attain the first 500 vertical feet, and it offers watered camping options for the multi-day ascent. Sabino Basin figures to be the easiest of the three routes. Still, it's a grind.

The first hurdle on the approach is financial. It's $10 to park at the Sabino Canyon parking lot overnight, and another $8 per person to ride the shuttle to the end of the canyon road.

From the end of the shuttle line, the trail makes a switchbacking climb for about 350' vertical feet to the north, and then traverses for 2 miles to Sabino Basin. Large cairns indicate the West Fork Sabino Trail heading upstream along beautiful Sabino Creek. It is 1.6 miles through the basin to Hutch's Pool. There are many fine campsites in the area where a base camp might be established for the full-day summit attempt.

Beyond Hutch's Pool, the West Fork Trail sees less use as it climbs through a saddle, and then winds along grassy slopes above the West Fork of Sabino Creek. The cairned trail leaves the slopes to drop into the drainage at 4,400', just upstream from where semi-permanent water surfaces in the

The twin summits of Cathedral Rock

West Fork. Shade from oaks, pines, and cypress now shelters the trail as it weaves up the canyon bottom.

There is a trail sign for the Cathedral Rock Trail at: N 32°23.443' W 110°49.566'. Cairns also indicate this junction of the Cathedral Rock and Romero Pass Trails, located under cover of forest, nearly 3.5 miles from Hutch's Pool.

The fading Cathedral Rock Trail climbs via switchbacks through burned slopes on the south side of the West Fork canyon. Cairns sometimes indicate the old overgrown trail, and sometimes point to new routes that avoid deadfall or thick brush. At 6,100' near the top of a ridge buttress, the cairned trail fades to obscurity. Fortunately, the best route is up the ridge to the west of the old trail anyway. Brush conditions are light to moderate.

At a bench at 6,600', the old trail re-emerges before vanishing for good in a brushy basin to the south. The quickest way to the double crowns of Cathedral Rock, which is now close at hand, continues up the ridge, and then veers southeast to intersect a cairned route coming from the Esperero Canyon saddle.

If you are intent on reaching the easiest 4th class route to the top, you'll have to angle across the burned basin below Cathedral Rock's east face. Aim for a saddle north of the peak (in heavy brush), then climb the northeast face over broken slabs and across brushy traverses to a sub-summit notch. From here, a couple of mantle moves lead to the crenelated slabs of the summit.

The cleanest route to the top approaches the peak from the south. This cairned route along the Esperero Canyon divide leads through a window notch towards the south end of a wall-fin that runs south from the summits. Once through the window notch, cairns lead through a granite wonderland before reaching two fifth class routes on the west side of the higher north summit. One is a short 5.4 face into a chimney traverse. The other, 100 feet farther north along the base of the cliffs, is a 5.1 sloping crack, often with ropes in it.

Many of the usual suspects are visible from the top, including Four Peaks to the north, Picacho Peak to the west, Wrightson Peak and mountains of Old Mexico in the south, and Dos Cabezas and the Chiricahuas to the east.

Take your photo and start back for camp, because this is a long day. If you reached the summit, you relied more on your own wits and determination than on this guidebook. Don't get benighted!!

Access: From the north, exit I-10 at Ina Road on the outskirts of Tucson and take Ina until it becomes Sunrise Drive. Follow Sunrise Drive east until it ends at Sabino Canyon Road. Take a left at Sabino Canyon Road, and a quick right into the Sabino Canyon visitor center.

From downtown Tucson, travel east to Craycroft, north to Sunrise Drive, and east again to Sabino Canyon Road and the visitor center.

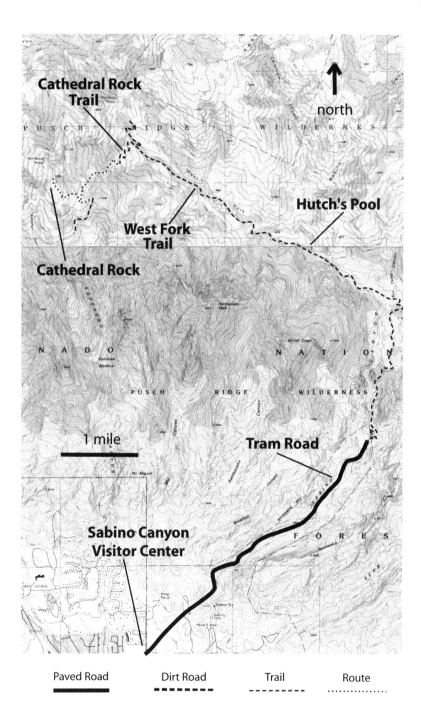

Cathedral Rock Trail

West Fork Trail

Hutch's Pool

Cathedral Rock

north

Tram Road

Sabino Canyon Visitor Center

1 mile

Paved Road   Dirt Road   Trail   Route

Mazatzal Peak

HIKE / SCRAMBLE

General Description: A full day hike to the high point of the rugged Mazatzal Mountains
Summit Elevation: 7,903'
Vertical Gain: 3,700'
Round-Trip Distance: 18 miles via Barnhardt Trail to Davenport Trail and northwest ridge / 14 miles via Barnhardt Trail to Suicide Ridge Route / 10 miles via Y Bar Trail and southeast ridge
Optimal Season: April — May, late September — November / Snow often covers the peak in winter. Summers are hot with occasional lightning.
Route Surface and Difficulty: Maintained trail / moderate brush off-trail hiking / 3rd class scrambling (4th class scrambling on southeast ridge route)

Mazatzal — Mah'zat sal. The word originated from southern Mexico's Aztecs, meaning "an area inhabited by deer." Its presence here could be an indication of far reaching trade routes that overlapped the Aztecs with people living in Arizona. The mountains are a significant feature of central Arizona. Their bedrock cliffs rise over the Tonto Basin to the east, form a wilderness surrounding the Verde River in the west, and border the Phoenix metropolis to the south. The range is vintage Arizona, a mix of pine and cactus, broiling deserts and lush grottoes. Mazatzal Peak is their high point, and several options exist for reaching its summit.

All routes begin at the Barnhardt Trailhead. The shortest route follows the Y Bar Trail south across the eastern slopes of the range. About 4 miles from the trailhead, Shake Tree Saddle is reached in open burned countryside between Shake Tree Canyon and Y Bar Basin. From the saddle, one can strike directly up slopes to the northwest, scrambling through blocky low cliffbands before emerging onto open gentle hillsides flanking the summit. Although this route is the most direct, the trail has occasional encroaching brush, and route finding through rocky bluffs can be challenging—class 4 in places.

More commonly used routes follow the Barnhardt Trail. The Barnhardt traverses steep north facing slopes above a rugged gorge that rumbles with waterfalls in spring. About 2 miles from the end of the road, the trail turns south into a steep tributary canyon, and climbs through maroon cliffs incised with ephemeral waterfalls. Nearly 4 miles from the trailhead, the trail rounds a ridge, and a basin at the head of Barnhardt Canyon unfolds to the west.

Cairns here indicate the Suicide Ridge Route, which is the most direct way to the summit from the Barnhardt Trail. Hikers should expect a moderate

Mazatzal Peak following a storm

grade and ample brush on the long rolling route, which doesn't actually merge with Suicide Ridge until 7,200' on the gentle upper mountain. The easiest access to the ridge route is not from the first cairns, but rather from the Sandy Saddle Trail junction, located another half-mile up the Barnhardt Trail at GPS: N34°05.275' W111°27.516'

Beyond the Sandy Saddle Trail junction, the Barnhardt Trail contours for another mile into a broad basin, and crosses a drainage of loose cobbles. Cairns indicate the obscured trail where it crosses the broad drainage, and enters a zone of fallen burned trees. Several tall ponderosa pines are still standing, poised to topple. I'd recommend passing the widowmakers with alacrity, especially on a windy day.

Once past the deadfall zone, mountaineers can start looking for routes to the northwest ridge, which offers the mellowest ascent to the top of Mazatzal Peak. There is a little-used route that leaves the trail amid ancient burned junipers a quarter-mile past the deadfall zone (GPS N34°05.028' W111°28.103'), and another that departs up a gully about 0.75 miles past the widowmakers (N34°04.933' W111°28.400'). If you've come this far, however, you might as well continue to the Davenport Trail junction on the Mazatzal Divide. This is the easiest way to gain the Northwest Ridge, by heading south along the range divide. Whichever route you decide to take, expect some brush and at least one steep slope en route. Craggy viewpoints within a half-mile of the summit offer better overlooks than the summit itself, although the view from the top is most excellent too.

From the top one can see the Mogollon Rim, the San Francisco Peaks, the Bradshaw Mountains, and whoa! is that a giant fountain spewing water into the atmosphere far below? A climb to the top of Mazatzal Peak is sure to provide a full day of foot travel through a uniquely Arizonan landscape, for worse, and for better.

Aceess: Take Highway 87 south from Payson or north from Mesa, and turn west onto road #419 toward the Barnhardt Trail. This road leaves the highway just south of Rye Creek, a few miles north of the Highway 188 junction. Follow road #419 for 4.8 dirt miles (muddy when wet) to the trailhead.

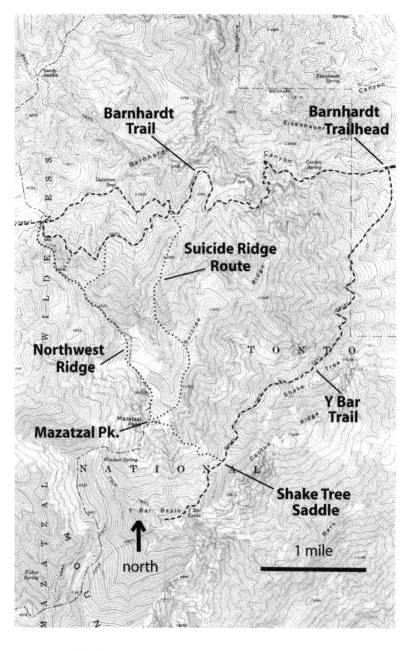

Barnhardt Trail

Barnhardt Trailhead

Suicide Ridge Route

Northwest Ridge

Y Bar Trail

Mazatzal Pk.

Shake Tree Saddle

north

1 mile

| Paved Road | Dirt Road | Trail | Route |

CLIMBS

Eagletail Peak

CLIMB

General Description: A technical rock climb in dramatic desert crags
Summit Elevation: 3,300'
Vertical Gain: 1,820'
Round-Trip Distance: 8 miles via shortcut route / 11 miles via long route
Optimal Season: November — March
Route Surface and Difficulty: Basic trail / off-trail desert with moderate brush / class 3 semi-loose scree / 4th class gully / 5.8 x 50' rock climb

Almost the entire Eagletail Mountain Range is a craggy jumble of spires and buttes. The high point of the range, Eagletail Peak, matches this profile perfectly, and it is the most difficult route in this book—if you go to the summit. Fortunately for non-climbers, there is a point near the true summit that offers equally impressive views without the trouble of climbing to the tippy top.

Regardless of your destination, virtually all access into the eastern Eagletail Mountains begins on an old jeep trail turned hiking trail. The trail follows a wash supporting ironwood and palo verde trees as it gradually climbs to a low pass beneath brilliant multi-hued cliffs. The terrain is flat. You'll have to pay attention to notice the actual pass crest, when the trail begins descending westward into a broad valley.

At this point, there are two route options. The flattest route follows the trail west for about 2 miles until beyond the last of some low hills that guard the main Eagletail uplift. Once past these low hills, near a flat-topped black mesa, the route veers northeast, and heads upstream to the base of an approach gully.

For the shorter cross-country route, stop at the low pass beneath the multi-hued cliffs. Look for another pass that we'll call Gateway Pass, located southwest of the Eagletail Peak massif. From the trail, Gateway Pass is easily spotted by first finding a dark cliffband below and left of Eagletail Peak. Trace this cliffband to the west and your eye will lead to Gateway Pass sitting in line with the shoulder of the mountain. To reach Gateway Pass, travel north from the trail across mostly flat terrain incised with shallow drainages, then continue up a gradual slope to the pass. From Gateway Pass, head slightly west of due north across the basin, aiming for a saddle that sits between the main mountain and a steep knoll with small rocky buttresses.

With either approach, the goal is to end up in a broad rocky approach gully that leads up the south side of the mountain toward a high saddle. This gully is the biggest grunt of the ascent, with class 3 hiking and scram-

Lunch break at the saddle on Eagletail Peak

bling over flaky bedrock and scree.

At the top, a shallow steep basin leads upward past shelter caves until feeding into a steep chute. The chute is loose, and often shaded, as it faces northwest down the spine of the range. A couple hundred feet of scrambling will have you out of the loose chute, and on an airy saddle with a view of the nearby summit.

From the top of the chute, non-technical climbers will want to make a short scramble to the left, and a breezy sub-summit. Those up for a 5.8 climb will continue to the base of the summit pinnacle, where an old belay bolt signals the base of the 5th class climbing pitch.

The climb leads about 50 feet up an exposed crack with loose rocks here and there. Fortunately, the crack provides ample holds away from the chossy rock, and decent protection can be placed in the crack too. There were two old but good fixed nuts in place on our ascent. Several small to medium nuts and some small to medium cams should be an adequate rack for the pitch.

The summit is a sharp and loose triple peak, with the middle rock pile being the highest. Between a chill wind and ghastly exposure, I didn't take time to scan the landscape for points of interest, but rest assured, the view is spectacular.

There is an 80' rappel off the summit that uses bolts on the northeast side of the pinnacle. While here, climbers might also consider scampering up the skinny "tail feathers" of Eagletail Peak. One of them is supposedly a spectacular 5.3 route.

Access: Take Interstate 10 west to exit #81 for Salome Highway. Go left over the freeway, and turn right on Harquahala Valley Road. Follow this paved road west, then south for about 11 miles to a T intersection at Baseline Road. Make a left at Baseline, then a quick right, again onto Harquahala Valley Road. In another mile, turn west toward the mountains on Eagle Tail Road, and follow this 4 miles to its end. Turn left onto a gas line road, and travel 0.3 miles south, crossing a wash en route. Turn west through a gate (close the gate!) at a cattle chute, and proceed on this wilderness access road for a little over a mile before branching right at a north-bound fork. Follow this two-track toward a low pass. It is just over 2 miles to road's end at the Eagle Tail Mountain wilderness boundary.

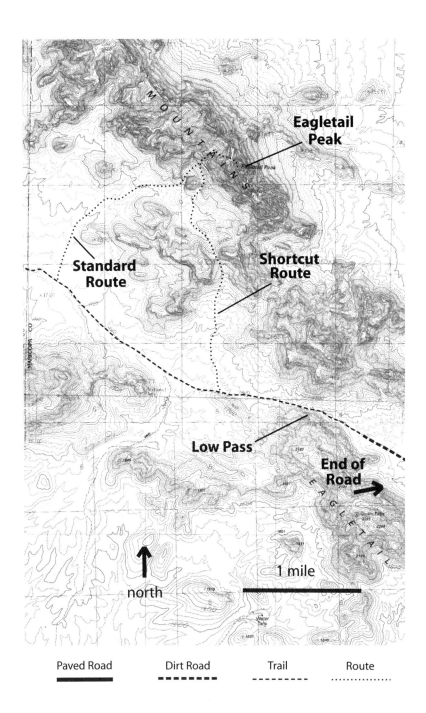

Baboquivari Peak

CLIMB

General Description: A rock climb up southern Arizona's most impressive summit
Summit Elevation: 7,730'
Vertical Gain: 3,400'
Round-Trip Distance: 8 miles
Optimal Season: April — May, late September — November
Route Surface and Difficulty: Steep use trail with moderate brush / cairned route on 3rd class rock / three 5th class climbs / use trail in heavy brush

"This is the one"
James Dickey's Lewis Medlock

Baboquivari is the most visible formation in southern Arizona. The sharks tooth spire is a beacon of the Sonoran Desert, and adventurers have been drawn to the peak for eons. The Toohno O'odham call the peak Waw Kiwu-lik. It's the center of their emergence into this world, and the sacred home of their God I'itoi. In 1968, Bill Forrest invented the modern climbing harness while projecting the peak's East Face route. It was 1898 when the first documented ascent of Babo took place. Doctor Forbes from the University of Arizona was the protagonist, finally reaching the top on his third attempt. The route he forged is the one described here, known honorably as the Forbes Route.

The route begins in Thomas Canyon southeast of the towering peak, where a dirt road leads through a white gate before bypassing a house and corral. The route is signed. Not far past the ranch home, the route narrows to a lightly cairned trail that is obscured by grass and brush, and sometimes blocked by deadfall. The trail crosses the creek a couple of times, but generally stays west of the drainage until about the 5,300' elevation, where it exits the creekbed and begins to climb a slope northeast of the canyon bottom. This important exit from the creekbed among large boulders in the steepening drainage is at GPS: N31°46.100' W111°35.337'. Don't leave the creek too soon on an immigrant trail in the oaks at 5,100'. I know from experience that this route only leads to the dike ridge east of Thomas Canyon! The climber's trail, on the other hand, climbs steeply toward tuff cliffs before traversing west into oak forest, and then climbing again to the obvious wooded saddle northeast of the peak.

From the forested saddle, find a path leading west, and upward. The route is steep, with chunky loose angular cobbles poised to roll. The forest

Babo

on this north side of the peak is shady and cool, with patches of poison ivy perilously close to the trail. Just before hitting the cliff of Babo, the route traverses right onto slickrock, and then follows the bottom of the cliff. Kitt Peak and the rugged flanks of the Baboquivari Range come into view.

Above, an obvious crooked gunsight notch signals the first climb—an awkward (5.3) move behind a chokestone wedged in a cave-like chimney. Bolts at the top of the route provide a belay anchor, but like all the pitches on the Forbes Route, no fixed protection is available for the lead climber, and the rock is not conducive to placed nuts or cams. The leader should count on climbing without protection.

Once above this first short pitch, continue along the base of the cliff 100 yards to the top of a brushy slope, and the bottom of pitch two. A seemingly bald bulging face creates an intimidating line, but bucket holds make it easier than it looks (5.2). Again, there are bolts on the sloping face above. (Rappelling from these bolts on a 200' rope leaves you 20' from the bottom. Count on downclimbing the final part of the pitch, or bring a longer rope.)

Above the second pitch, don't be lured left to daylight. Rather, traverse right 75 yards on a vague trail leading through an oak thicket. The top of this forested gully is the base of the third, or "Ladder" pitch. This final climb is easily recognizable by the remnants of a metal and wood ladder that was once anchored here. There are bolts at the halfway point, and also at the top of this 70' pitch (5.3).

Traverse right through vegetation once more and scramble around a chokestone to gain a U-shaped gulch of loose rock. The trail re-emerges here, and leads left and up toward the summit. Head-high brush encroaches on the route a hundred feet below the top, one final obstacle en route to the sacred summit.

The view is stunning, extending far into Mexico. Gifts for I'itoi adorn the high point. Unless you made a truly alpine start, the sun will be well over the Pacific by the time you enjoy this expansive vista. With three rappels and a steep trail still ahead on the return, it's little wonder why so many parties have spent an impromptu night in the bush under the spell of Babo.

Access: From Tucson, head west on Highway 86—Ajo Highway—about 20 miles to Highway 286. Take lonely 286 south about 29.5 miles to milepost 15.8, and turn right at a mailbox. Proceed through a gate (Of course, close all gates along the route.), and continue 2.6 miles before forking right at a "Mormon Corrals" sign. This secondary dirt road heads northeast for 0.3 miles before curving back toward the west, and Baboquivari. At 3.5 miles from the highway, proceed through a second gate, and yet another at 5.5 miles. The road gets rockier past here, but it is still passable to a well driven high clearance 2WD. At a hill crest 7.1 miles from the highway, a sign indicates no camping beyond this point. There are two nice campsites here, at GPS: N31°44.549' W111°34.449'. In the valley below is an old windmill and some sycamore trees. Above looms the hulking pinnacle of Baboquivari. If you are not camping, you may proceed another kilometer (0.62 miles) to a white gate before parking.

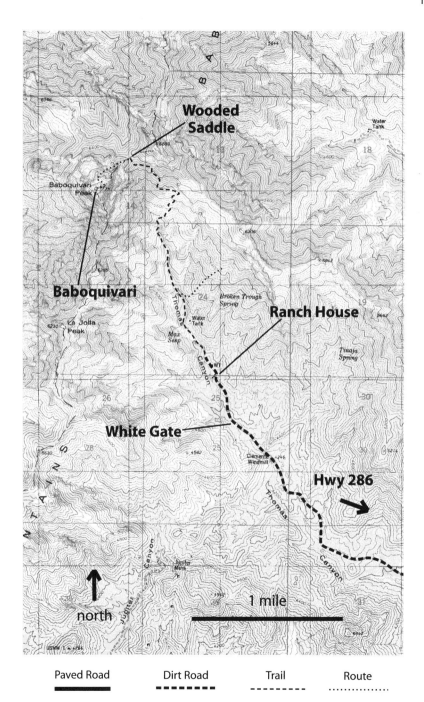

Wooded Saddle

Baboquivari

Ranch House

White Gate

Hwy 286

north

1 mile

| Paved Road | Dirt Road | Trail | Route |

Weavers Needle

CLIMB

General Description: A hike and climb to the top of the Superstition Mountain's most iconic landmark
Summit Elevation: 4,553'
Vertical Gain: 2,720'
Round-Trip Distance: 8 miles
Optimal Season: October — April
Route Surface and Difficulty: Trail / 2nd & 3rd class slope / one-pitch rock climb (5.3) / 4th class scramble

Weavers Needle was named after one of Arizona's most noted outdoorsmen, Pauline Weaver, who roamed the territory in the mid-1800s. The dramatic spire is said to cast a shadow on the legendary Lost Dutchman Mine. Attempts at climbing the peak in the 1960s were hindered by eccentric gold seekers who guarded the Needle and its alleged buried riches. Today the area is more tame, but a climb up Weaver's remains a classic Arizona adventure.

There are a couple ways to approach Weavers Needle. The one described here is the most easily accessed, beginning at the Peralta Trailhead. The Peralta Trail follows Peralta Canyon upstream from the parking area, crossing the creekbed a couple times as it weaves through impenetrable pockets of desert scrub. Outrageous rock formations, including rock windows, line ridge tops above the canyon. The trail reaches the head of the canyon at Fremont Saddle 2.5 miles from the road. Weavers Needle bursts into view.

Access to the Needle continues down the trail into East Boulder Canyon for a little over a mile before leaving the trail for a use-route that heads to the base of the spire. The cairned route leaves the trail just beyond the last hoodoo pinnacles, at N33°25.756' W111°22.566'.

After crossing the bed of Boulder Canyon and heading through some brush, the route leads up a boulder strewn slope towards the Needle. Near the base of the Needle cliffs, a rocky outcrop is bypassed to the left as the route enters a shady bedrock gully.

The gully quickly steepens to 4th class. After about a hundred feet of scrambling (with one bolt and an old steel pipe for anchors), the route gets steeper. Spotty protection comes via cracks for mid-sized gear. The crux comes just below a chockstone at the top, where a heady 5.5 face move to the right can be supplanted with an easier crawl beneath the boulder.

Once atop the chokestone, the crux is behind you, but lots of 4th class and a couple vertical sections still remain. A 12' wall with huge holds comes

Off route en route to Weavers Needle

next, and then more class 3 and 4 scrambling leads to a final thirty foot cliff. This final obstacle (5.2) has bolt anchors at the top. An easy walk from here leads a short way to the summit.

There is a slightly easier route leading to the crux chockstone from the east. This option offers a 5.3 face climb with spotty protection options low in the route, followed by a 4th class scramble to the chockstone. To reach the east side route, simply traverse along the base of the Needle cliffs from the west approach until reaching the moderate route.

A 200' rope and a few medium stoppers are recommended gear for the Weavers Needle. Helmets never hurt either.

Access: From Apache Junction, AZ, take Highway 60 southeast for about 8 miles, and turn north onto road #77 near milepost 204. Follow road #77 to its end at the Peralta Trailhead in 7.2 miles. There is no camping at the trailhead.

Agave

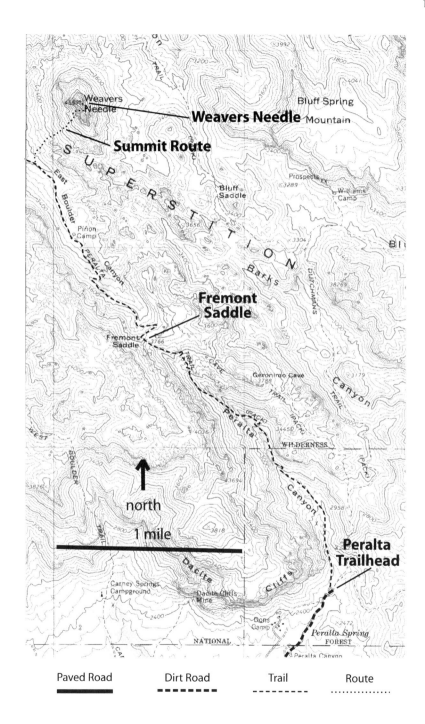

Paved Road	Dirt Road	Trail	Route

The 50 State High Points

Elevation

1	AK	Denali	20,320'
2	CA	Mt. Whitney	14,491'
3	CO	Mt. Elbert	14,433'
4	WA	Mt. Rainier	14,410'
5	WY	Gannett Pk.	13,804'
6	HI	Mauna Kea	13,796'
7	UT	Kings Pk.	13,528'
8	NM	Wheeler Pk.	13,161'
9	NV	Boundary Pk.	13,140'
10	MT	Granite Pk.	12,799'
11	ID	Borah Pk.	12,662'
12	AZ	Humphreys PK.	12,633'
13	OR	Mt. Hood	11,239'
14	TX	Guadalupe Pk.	8,749'
15	SD	Hamey Pk.	7,242'
16	NC	Mt. Mitchell	6,684'
17	TN	Clingmans Dome	6,643'
18	NH	Mt. Washington	6,288'
19	VA	Mt. Rogers	5,729'
20	NE	Panorama Pt.	5,426'
21	NY	Mt. Marcy	5,344'
22	ME	Katahdin	5,268'
23	OK	Black Mesa	4,973'
24	WV	Spruce Knob	4,861'
25	GA	Brasstown Bald	4,783'
26	VT	Mt. Mansfield	4,393'
27	KY	Black Mtn.	4,139'
28	KS	Mt. Sunflower	4,039'
29	SC	Sassafras Mtn.	3,554'
30	ND	White Butte	3,506'
31	MA	Mt. Greylock	3,488'
32	MD	Backbone Mtn.	3,360'
33	PA	Mt. Davis	3,213'
34	AR	Magazine Mtn.	2,753'
35	AL	Cheaha Mtn.	2,405'
36	CT	Mt. Frissell	2,372'
37	MN	Eagle Mtn.	2,301'
38	MI	Mt. Arvon	1,978'
39	WI	Timms Hill	1,951'
40	NJ	High Point	1,803'
41	MO	Taum Sauk Mtn.	1,772'
42	IA	Hawkeye Point	1,670'
43	OH	Capbell Hill	1,549'
44	IN	Hoosier Hill	1,257'
45	IL	Charles Mound	1,235'
46	RI	Jerimoth Hill	812'
47	MS	Woodall Mtn.	806'
48	LA	Driskill Mtn.	535'
49	DL	Ebright Azimuth	442'
50	FL	Britton Hill	345'

United States' 50 most prominent peaks

			Prominence	Elevation
1	Mt. Rainier	WA	13,197'	14,410'
2	Mt. Whitney	CA	10,075'	14,495'
3	Mt. Shasta	CA	9,762'	14,162'
4	Mt. Elbert	CO	9,073'	14,433'
5	Mt. Baker	WA	8,881'	10,781'
6	San Jacinto Pk.	CA	8,311'	10,831'
7	San Gorgonio	CA	8,282'	11,502'
8	Charleston Pk.	NV	8,243'	11,918'
9	Mt. Adams	WA	8,116'	12,276'
10	Mt. Olympus	WA	7,829	7,869'
11	Mt. Hood	OR	7,679'	11,239'
12	Wheeler Pk.	NV	7,563'	13,063'
13	Glacier Pk.	WA	7,480'	10,520'
14	White Mtn. Pk.	CA	7,196'	14,246'
15	Gannett Pk.	WY	7,074'	13,804'
16	Cloud Pk.	WY	7,067'	13,167'
17	Grand Teton	WY	6,530'	13,770'
18	Sacajawea Pk.	OR	6,388'	9,838'
19	Kings Pk.	UT	6,348'	13,528'
20	Mt. Graham	AZ	6,340'	10,720'
21	Mt. San Antonio	CA	6,224'	10,064'
22	Telescope Pk.	CA	6,168'	11,048'
23	Mt. Peale	UT	6,161'	12,721'
24	Mt. Washington	NH	6,138'	6,288'
25	Mt. Mitchell	NC	6,089'	6,684'
26	Humphreys Pk.	AZ	6,039'	12,633'
27	Borah Pk.	ID	5,982'	12,662'
28	Mt. Jefferson	NV	5,861'	11,941'
29	Mt. Ellen	UT	5,842'	11,522'
30	Deseret Pk.	UT	5,811'	11,031'
31	Mt. Jefferson	OR	5,777'	10,497'
32	Pilot Pk.	NV	5,726'	10,716'
33	Crazy Pk.	MT	5,709'	11,209'
34	McDonald Pk.	MT	5,640'	9,820'
35	South Sister	OR	5,578'	10,358'
36	Sierra Blanca Pk.	NM	5,533'	11,973'
37	Pikes Pk.	CO	5,510'	14,110'
38	Mt. Nebo	UT	5,488'	11,928'
39	Snowshoe Pk.	MT	5,418'	8,738'
40	North Schell Pk.	MT	5,403'	11,883'
41	Star Pk.	NV	5,396'	9,836'
42	Hayford Pk.	NV	5,392'	9,912'
43	Diamond Pk.	ID	5,377'	12,197'
44	Flat Top Mtn.	UT	5,370'	10,620'
45	Mt. Stuart	WA	5,335'	9,415'
46	Blanca Pk	CO	5,305'	14,345'
47	Mt. Timpanogos	UT	5,270'	11,750'
48	Ibapah Pk.	UT	5,269'	12,109'
49	Lassen Pk.	CA	5,229'	10,457'
50	Mt. Cleveland	MT	5,226'	10,466'

Arizona's 50 Highest Points (minimum 500' prominence)

7.5 topographic maps in parenthesis
Quotations indicate unofficial names to unnamed peaks

1	Humphreys Pk.	12,633'	(Humphreys Pk.)
2	Agassiz Pk.	12,356'	(Humphreys Pk.)
3	Fremont Pk.	11,969'	(Humphreys Pk.)
4	Doyle Pk.	11,460'	(Humphreys Pk.)
5	Mt. Baldy	11,420'	(Mt. Baldy)
6	Mt. Ord	11,357'	(Mt. Baldy)
7	Paradise Butte	11,150'	(Mt. Baldy)
8	Escudilla Mtn.	10,912'	(Escudilla Mtn.)
9	Mt. Graham	10,720'	(Mt. Graham)
10	Kendrick Pk.	10,418'	(Kendrick Pk.)
11	Greens Pk.	10,133'	(Greens Pk.)
12	Webb Pk.	10,030'	(Webb Pk.)
13	Heliograph PK.	10,022'	(Mt. Graham)
14	Burnt Mtn.	9,970'	(Bonito Rock)
15	Chiricahua Pk.	9,796'	(Chiricahua Pk.)
16	Pole Knoll	9,793'	(Greens Pk.)
17	Roof Butte	9,783'	(Roof Butte)
18	St. Peters Dome	9,636'	(Whiting Knoll)
19	"SE Roof Butte"	9,566'	(Roof Butte)
20	Matthews Pk.	9,550'	(Tsaile)
21	Miller Pk.	9,466'	(Miller Pk.)
22	"View Pt. Mtn."	9,466'	(Cove)
23	"Lukachukai So."	9,460'	(Lukachukai)
24	Mt. Wrightson	9,453'	(Mt. Wrightson)
25	Pastora Pk.	9,407'	(Pastora Pk.)
26	"Bear High Pt."	9,396'	(Tsaile Butte)
27	Sitgreaves Mtn.	9,388'	(Sitgreaves Mtn.)
28	Mt. Elden	9,299'	(Flagstaff East)
29	Sugarloaf Mtn.	9,283'	(Sunset Crater West)
30	"Big Lake Mtn."	9,269'	(Lukachukai)
31	Bill Williams Mtn.	9,264'	(Williams So.)
32	Boundary Butte	9,263'	(Boundary Butte)
33	Carr Pk.	9,230'	(Miller Pk.)
34	Aspen Butte	9,215'	(Bonito Rock)
35	"West Twin"	9,190'	(Escudilla Mtn.)
36	Kaibab Plateau	9,176'	(DeMotte Park)
37	Cerro Gordo	9,161'	(Boundary Butte)
38	Mt. Lemmon	9,157'	(Mt. Lemmon)
39	Tsaile Butte	9,128'	(Tsaile Butte)
40	Antelope Mtn.	9,003'	(Greer)
41	Lukachukai Mtn.	8,947'	(MX Cry Mesa)
42	Blue Jay Pk.	8,860'	(Blue Jay Pk.)
43	Mica Mtn.	8,664'	(Mica Mtn.)
44	Cerro Trigo	8,614'	(Whiting Knoll)
45	Mt. Hopkins	8,585'	(Mt. Hopkins)
46	Mt. Bigelow	8,540'	(Mt. Bigelow)
47	Hutch Mtn.	8,532'	(Hutch Mtn.)
48	Mormon Mtn.	8,510'	(Mormon Mtn.)
49	Lake Mtn.	8,501'	(Sponseller Mtn.)
50	Rincon Pk.	8,482'	(Rincon Pk.)

Arizona's top 50 peaks in prominence

		Prominence	Elevation	
1	Mt. Graham	6,340′	10,720′	(Mt. Graham)
2	Humphreys Pk.	6,039′	12,633′	(Humphreys Pk.)
3	Mt. Lemmon	5,177′	9,157′	(Mt. Lemmon)
4	Chiricahua Pk.	5,149′	9,796′	(Chiricahua Pk.)
5	Miller Pk.	5,011′	9,466′	(Miller Pk.)
6	Baldy Pk.	4,728′	11,420′	(Mt. Baldy)
7	Mica Mtn.	4,604′	8,664′	(Mica Mtn.)
8	Mt. Wrightson	4,591′	9,453′	(Mt. Wrightson)
9	Hualapai Pk.	4,447′	8,417′	(Hualapai Pk.)
10	Baboquivari Pk.	4,204′	7,734′	(Baboquivari Pk.)
11	Pinal Pk.	4,086′	7,848′	(Pinal Pk.)
12	Mazatzal Pk.	3,963′	7,903′	(Mazatzal Pk.)
13	Mt. Tipton	3,638′	7,148′	(Mt. Tipton)
14	Kaibab Plateau	3,610′	9,176′	(DeMotte Park)
15	Mt. Turnbull	3,582′	8,282′	(Mt. Turnbull)
16	Signal Pk.	3,487′	4,877′	(Palm Canyon)
17	Harquahala Mtn.	3,471′	5,681′	(Harquahala Mtn.)
18	Browns Pk.	3,317′	7,657′	(Four Peaks)
19	Dos Cabezas	3,244′	8,357′	(Dos Cabezas)
20	Mt. Wilson	3,225′	5,445′	(Mt. Wilson)
21	Sierra Estrella Pk.	3,217′	4,512′	(Avondale SE)
22	Roof Butte	3,170′	9,783′	(Roof Butte)
23	Bassett Pk.	3,133′	7,663′	(Bassett Pk.)
24	Crossman Pk.	3,120′	5,100′	(Crossman Pk.)
25	Mt. Trumbull	2,974′	8,038′	(Mt. Trumbull)
26	Mt. Union	2,949′	7,982′	(Groom Creek)
27	Woodchute Mtn.	2,930′	7,860′	(Munds Draw)
28	Mt. Bangs	2,912′	8,016′	(Mt. Bangs)
29	Mt. Glenn	2,899′	7,500′	(Cochise Stronghold)
30	Apache Pk.	2,897′	7,711′	(Apache Pk.)
31	Harvcuvar Mtn - Smith Pk.	2,797′	5,242′	(Smith Pk.)
32	Pastora Pk.	2,707′	9,407′	(Pastora Pk.)
33	Mt. Ajo	2,703′	4,808′	(Mt. Ajo)
34	Mt. Ballard	2,680′	7,370′	(Bisbee)
35	Gu Achi	2,646′	4,556′	(Santa Rosa Mtns. SW)
36	Apache Pks.	2,600′	6,940′	(Chrome Butte)
37	Newman Pk.	2,531′	4,508′	(Newman Pk.)
38	White Tank Mtns.	2,523′	4,083′	(White Tank Mtns.)
39	Pinnacle Ridge	2,490′	7,550′	(Buford Hill)
40	Kendrick Pk.	2,488′	10,418′	(Kendrick Pk.)
41	Aztec Pk.	2,488′	7,748′	(Aztec Pk.)
42	Keystone Pk.	2,458′	6,188′	(Sanamiego Pk.)
43	Mt. Ord	2,428′	7,128′	(Reno Pass)
44	Guthrie Pk.	2,401′	6,571′	(Guthrie)
45	Maple Pk.	2,394′	8,294′	(Maple Pk.)
46	Escudilla Mtn.	2,382′	10,912′	(Escudilla Mtn.)
47	Reiley Pk.	2,360′	7,631′	(Reiley Pk.)
48	Coyote Pk.	2,349′	2,808′	(Wellton SE)
49	Table Top	2,338′	4,373′	(Indian Butte)
50	Sheep Mtn.	2,331′	3,156′	(Wellton Hills)

156

When FIT Matters Most

ASOLO
www.asolo.com

Author Tyler Williams used Power Matic 200 gv Asolo boots during research for this book. They survived many sharp desert miles.

Thanks to Pinnacle Mapping Technologies for help with *Arizona Summits* maps

OSPREY.

www.ospreypacks.com

Talon 44

Multi-day
Adventure

Pack Your Passion. Go.

Author Tyler Williams used Osprey packs during research for this book, as he
does on all his adventures.

Funhog Press also appreciates these sponsors

TEVA footwear
Bluewater ropes

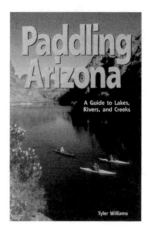

Both easy trails and technical gorges are covered in this complete guidebook. *Canyoneering Arizona* is a staple for adventuring in the Southwest.

Fisherman, birdwatchers, canoeists, touring kayakers, and whitewater boaters—this book is for you. *Paddling Arizona* is your key to finding water in Arizona.

www.funhogpress.com

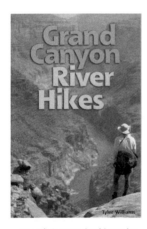

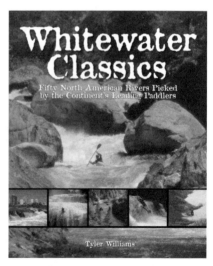

Grand Canyon junkies take notice! The Canyon's known destinations and hidden grottoes are both covered here. Eminence Break, The Tabernacle, Dox Castle... the list goes on.

If a whitewater paddler can have only one book, this should be it. "Classics" is part guide book and part history book, all in stunning color.

To order Funhog books

Tear out this page and send the
completed order form to:

Funhog Press
2819 N. Center St.
Flagstaff, AZ 86004

-or-

Visit: **www.funhogpress.com**

-or-

Ask for them at your local bookstore
or adventure outfitter.

Grand Canyon River Hikes	$18.95	_____
Canyoneering Arizona	$19.95	_____
Paddling Arizona	$19.95	_____
Arizona Summits South	$19.95	_____
Whitewater Classics	$26.95	_____

sub total	_____
AZ residents add 8.3% sales tax	_____
Shipping $3 for 1st book, $1 per additional	_____
Total	_____

Funhog Press is a small, independently owned publisher. We are dedicated
to the production of quality books with an original voice. Thank you for
your support.